the
imperfect
welcome

Praise for **The Imperfect Welcome**

"*The Imperfect Welcome* offers a fresh vision for belonging, making radical hospitality attainable for us all."

—**Dr. David Anderson**, Executive Director,
Lydia Home and Safe Families for Children

"In *The Imperfect Welcome*, Alysa Clark challenges our often-limiting view of hospitality and inspires us to offer up what we have—however imperfect—to radically love those around us. Her story-driven approach will expand your mind and enlarge your heart. She doesn't just tell us what to do—she leads by example."

—**Becky Baudouin**, speaker and author of
Enjoy Every Minute and Other Ridiculous Things We Say to Moms

"Alysa's hospitable, generous, and vibrant life oozes from every page as an inspiration to us all. A compelling call to imagine inhabiting a posture of inclusion and embrace, *The Imperfect Welcome* offers us a well worn path to emulate."

—**Beth Bruno**, author of *A Voice Becoming*

"From Genesis to Revelation, the Bible shows us that God is a God of hospitality who hospitably welcomes us into his family and calls us to share this same welcome with others. But this requires some courage, risk, and a willingness to even make mistakes. Alysa Clark's *The Imperfect Welcome* is a rich account of one family's attempts to live out God's hospitality. These stories will encourage you to take some risks and will show you both the joys and challenges that can come out of seeking to live out of God's hospitality."

—**Joshua Jipp**, PhD, Professor of New Testament
at Trinity Evangelical Divinity School,
author of *Saved by Faith and Hospitality*

"Chapter seven is titled 'I See You' and it completely embodies the heart of Alysa and her family. In a world that is reeling with hurt, greed, and isolation, the stories you read about radical hospitality will inspire you to open your heart and home to those around you. I Peter 4:9 encourages us to 'cheerfully share with others.' My prayer is that each one of us will be challenged to offer hospitality in fresh ways as a result of reading *The Imperfect Welcome*."

—**Amy Robnik Joob**, coach, speaker, and author of
Model Behavior: Make Your Career Path Your Calling
and *Unstuck: Step into the New*

"A thoughtful, challenging, heart-felt book from beginning to end."

—**Melissa Parks**, Editorial Director at CZ Strategy,
Co-Founder of Journey Sixty6

"I loved reading Alysa's journey of creating an "environment of belonging" both with her life and with this book. From chapter to chapter, it is wrapped in goodness, hope, and an invitation to live a life of hospitality. I am challenged to be both the one opening my door in welcome and to be the one stepping through an unknown threshold."

—**Christina Quist**, Founder of the not-for-profit community
Havilah Collective and author of *Kaleidoscope:
absurdly short stories of traveling and unraveling*

the
imperfect
welcome

when an ordinary family,
eclectic strangers,
and radical hospitality collide

alysa clark

Library of Congress Control Number: 2023913678
ISBN (softcover) 979-8-9888034-0-9
ISBN (ebook) 979-8-9888034-1-6
ISBN (audio) 979-8-9888034-2-3
RELIGION / Christian Living / Inspirational

Cover art and design: Jack Clark
Interior design: David W. Edelstein

www.alysaclark.com

Printed in the United States of America

For Jack, Madison, and Jackson

These are our stories.

If anyone knows my imperfections,
it's the three of you;

and you love me anyway.

You have my heart.

Contents

the
imperfect
welcome

Author's Note

Friends,

What you hold in your hands is a piece of my heart, the seeds of this book dating back to my earliest childhood days.

The Imperfect Welcome is all I have ever known, even though I didn't have a name for it until recent years.

My parents left their home country (USA) to go to another country (Canada) as missionaries. My brother, Lenny, and I were born and raised in Canada, in a culture different from that of our parents.

My dad didn't have what you might call a normal job. He was an itinerant preacher who traveled all over northern Ontario. My stay-at-home mom spoke with a thick southern accent and served sweat tea to guests. She never surrendered that southern drawl, by the way. After all these years in the "north country," all it takes is a sentence or two from Mae Emma for someone to remark, "You're not from around here, are you?" And the name! I can't imagine how many times she's had to explain the (apparently) very southern concept of "two names for the price of one."

It was just the four of us. Lenny and I didn't grow up

spending time with cousins or grandparents or any other extended family. And I'm sure my parents felt pretty isolated themselves. But this is not a call for pity. Not in the least. Why?

Because of the Brideau family. They (among many others) realized we had no relatives to spend holidays with, so they included us in their get-togethers. When they planned a party of any kind, we got an invitation. Little by little our concept of "family" grew from the four of us to include a large number of people we weren't even related to! It was then that I learned a lesson that would shape my adult life. The people who welcome you in—invite you in—give you a place to belong and that's how you become family.

We all know what it's like to feel welcome—in a home or even in a circumstance. In the pages that follow I hope you will sense the joy and connection that is available for us all, simply by living a life of welcome.

I'm convinced there is no better way to live.

Lovingly,
Alysa

Disclaimer

While all stories in this book are true,
most names, event sequences,
and identifying details
have been changed to protect the privacy
of the people involved.

Introduction

"In a polarized climate where people feel more divided than ever, where they're incentivized to huddle up with those who think, look, and believe like they do, we have an opportunity to do the opposite—to welcome people in."

Rebekah Lyons

Sometimes, hospitality gets a bad rap. Like a *really* bad rap. And then throw the word 'radical' in front of it, and people run for the hills.

Radical *what?*

The Imperfect Welcome—radical hospitality—is so much more than setting a pretty table and offering a three-course meal on an Instagram-worthy tablescape. It is more than a scheduled time for someone to visit our curated, clean, and clutter-free homes. Rather, it's about letting others into our lives, our hearts, and our stories.

And that's exactly what I want to do for you through the pages of this book: let you into my life, my heart, and my story. I want to show you that hospitality can be sustainable. We'll address the fears and concerns that go along with being vulnerable, and hopefully, together, we can shift our thinking about hospitality being about something we do to hospitable being who we are.

> The goal of hospitality is connection— not perfection.

The good news? *The Imperfect Welcome* isn't about doing more. Since the "perfect" welcome is seldom achievable, much less sustainable, we get to relax and be our imperfect selves! We choose to welcome others into our spheres, with kindness and compassion. This is not a performance. It is presence.

Western culture drops a whole slew of ideas into one large bucket labeled hospitality, and then we feel overwhelmed by the size of that bucket! Somehow, over time, we have decided that hospitality was a woman's work, equated to time in a kitchen slaving over a fancy homemade meal. And then we added "must have spotless home" into the pot, which scares most of us silly. That feels exhausting. And that isn't hospitality.

Maybe you're thinking, "I can't make a fancy meal for people, I'm just not good at that." Or, "I don't like entertaining people because I'm introverted and need my alone time." Or maybe you think, "My house is too small, messy, outdated (fill in the blank), or life is so busy, I just don't have time to have people over."

Anything in the previous paragraph ring true for you? No judgment, because I've been there, too. The problem is that we have a preconceived idea of what hospitality is supposed to look like, and we tend to fixate on that instead of the "why." We complicate the why by worrying too much about the how.

The goal of hospitality is connection—not perfection. In fact, *imperfection* is pretty attractive because it takes our ego out of the equation, sets people at ease, and results in the mutual gift of a safe place for belonging.

In the pages that follow, my prayer is that we would be inspired to increasingly offer ourselves and all our imperfections to others, in the hopes that they, too, will offer themselves and all their imperfections to us in return.

We all need a place to belong.

May the reading of these stories reach a spot in your heart that you never knew was there. May they help you to connect with people in ways you wouldn't have thought possible.

Let me introduce you to a few of the folks whose lives, as they intertwined with mine, fostered the community and belonging I think we all long for.

01

Why Would You Let Me Live with You?

"How wonderful it is that no one has to wait, but can start right now to gradually change the world! How wonderful it is that everyone, great and small, can immediately help bring about justice by giving of themselves."

Anne Frank

Several months into our friendship, while sitting in our tiny backyard sharing chips and ham sandwiches, Darisa asked why we would let her, a stranger, live with our family.

In an awkward attempt at humor she chuckled and said, "You didn't know me at all. I could have murdered you in your sleep. I could have been anybody. There are crazy people out there, ya know!"

We laughed together, reminded that we really didn't know her *at all* when we welcomed her into our home, those many months prior.

Earlier that winter, my husband Jack and I were at a meeting of Safe Families for Children ("Safe Families"), a "global organization whose mission is to keep children safe and families together."[1] That night a single mom shared how volunteers were hosting her three-year-old daughter Anora while she was living in her taxi, searching for consistent work. After she shared pieces of her story, the emcee casually mentioned that Darisa was still, in fact, homeless. It was late January, with temperatures dipping into the low teens and, at the end of the meeting, she would head back to her car to sleep.

As the meeting went on and another person stood up to talk, I was lost in this woman's reality. It was 20°F outside, and within the hour she would head out to her taxi for the night. That didn't feel right.

I shifted in my seat, discreetly leaned forward in my chair, and caught my husband's eye, who happened to be across the room. With raised eyebrows, a nod of the head, and a mouthed *our house?* exchange, we decided to invite this stranger out of the cold and into our home.

After the meeting, we dodged people in the overcrowded fellowship hall to make our way to the front, hoping to meet her.

"Hi there, I'm Jack and this is my wife, Alysa. Wow. Thanks for sharing your story. Ummm, well. We don't live too far from here, and we know you don't know us, but … if you'd like, we would be happy for you to stay with us, to get out of the cold. We'd love to have you."

Darisa smiled with a pleasant, gracious smile that we learned to love. "That sounds so nice. I'm working tonight but I could come tomorrow morning. Would that be okay?"

We agreed, exchanged numbers, gave her our address, and slipped out as more people jockeyed to meet her.

We stepped out into the frigid air, chins down, shoulders braced against the bitter wind, as we made our way through the crowded parking lot. We shivered as we waited for the car to warm up, and as we sat in silence, it dawned on us. *We don't even know this lady or her background. What will the sleeping arrangements be? How long will she stay? Are we putting our kids at risk? Is she going to want to bring her daughter to our house, too? Do we give her a house key without knowing one thing about her?*

What did we just do?

We also wrestled with another inner voice that was concerned for Darisa. We wondered what would happen if we didn't invite her in. Would she continue to sleep in her taxi indefinitely? Could we help in such a way that she would be able to live with her daughter again? How could we *not* invite her in?

What's her story?

We felt the tension between our abundance and her

need. We had a home we could share; she was vulnerable. But we also had questions and wanted to be wise. It seemed that every question we raised about concerns with helping her was met with other questions that spoke to the "What if we don't help?" conundrum. She wasn't just a problem or a statistic on paper. She was a real person whose path crossed ours—a mom like me. She wanted the best for her daughter, but was struggling on her own.

When she arrived at our home late the next morning, she was weary and longed for rest. I showed her to her room and she slept soundly for seven hours, her first solid sleep in months.

"I can't even tell you how great it felt to sleep with soft blankets and a pillow. It was amazing to completely stretch my legs out and sleep on my stomach, without being curled up in the back seat of my car," she said after waking from a deep slumber mid-afternoon.

"Oh, I'm so tickled to hear that, Darisa. I can't even imagine how glorious that felt. We're so glad you're here. Please make yourself at home. Truly. Let me show you around the kitchen so you know where things are and if I'm not here and you need something, just dig around until you find it. You're welcome to whatever you find."

With newfound energy she opened cupboards and pulled out a plate and mug to make herself some toast and coffee before heading back out to work the evening rush hour.

"It feels so good to be back in a real kitchen with things

like a toaster and a microwave. I don't need much, but I've missed grabbing an easy meal before heading off to work."

In total, Darisa lived with us for seven months and over time, we learned pieces of her story. She was born and raised in Turkmenistan, a country in Central Asia, and came to America in 2001 to attend university. After graduating she started a job and sent most of her earnings back home, to provide for their needs, as many immigrants do.

When we met, she was a single mother, struggling to make ends meet, as her daughter's father skipped out on them when Anora was one. He occasionally called, but remained uninvolved and uninterested in supporting his child. In time, bills piled up, and they lost their apartment.

While living out of her taxi for months and keeping a gym membership so that she would have a place to shower, she stumbled across Safe Families. Through them she entrusted her daughter to a loving family so that she could work long hours, many of them overnight, in an effort to pay bills.

With impeccable timing, our basement flooded that first week Darisa stayed with us. Because our master bedroom is in the basement, and she was settled in our upstairs guest bedroom, Jack and I took to an air mattress on the living room floor, just inside our front door.

We would hear her key turn in the lock at, say, 3 a.m., and because Coco, our five-pound Morkie, tried to protect us like a Doberman, with yips that only the littlest of dogs can yip, our nights were arduous, too.

In desperation and in an effort to keep the kids asleep, I would hiss through clenched teeth, "Coco. STOP. It's okay. STOP. It's our friend. STOPPPPPPP."

"Sorry. So sorry, Miss Alysa and Mister Jack," Darisa would whisper as she side-stepped over the end of our mattress, tip-toeing upstairs to her room. (The first night she accidentally stepped on the mattress and launched me right off the side. Good times.)

This scenario was on repeat for the better part of a week.

We can laugh about it now—but in the moment it was hard.

Darisa was lovely to have around, and increasingly she joined in our family activities, whether it was a family movie night or grilling on Sunday afternoons. When she wasn't working, she fit right in, and it felt good to know we were helping her get back on her feet.

As weeks rolled by, through random comments she made, we realized Darisa was not saving much of the money she was earning. Though putting in long hours each day and night, there were frequent stops at restaurants, even though we had encouraged her to eat anything she found in our kitchen. She would casually mention the new Barbie she purchased for her daughter, or how they had stopped at the mall to "Build-A-Bear" so that Anora would have something to snuggle at night. While it was certainly understandable (we all want to give our kids good things), we were perplexed. We were sacrificing to have her in our home, yet it seemed her independence was no nearer than the day she first arrived.

Because we had some skin in the game (at this point she had lived with us for eight weeks), and because we had shown kindness and built credibility, we were able to have the let's-come-up-with-a-plan conversation.

"Hey Darisa, we would love to sit down and talk through your plans for moving back in with Anora," I said late one afternoon.

"Sure. I'm here for another hour until I head out for work. Want to talk now?"

We sat together at our dining room table as Jack led the discussion. While he validated her hard work ethic and her love for Anora, he reminded her that she was a great mom and that above all, Anora needed her. Daughters need their mothers.

He then placed one lone piece of printer paper on the table and near the top he wrote "One Goal: Darisa and Anora living together."

He drew a big box around the statement.

"I know how much you miss Anora, and you've told us many times that you can't wait until you're back together again," he said.

"Yes, I miss her so much, and I know she desperately misses me. I really want to live with her soon."

"I know it's hard, but I think for that to happen, you might need to stop sending as much money back to your family every month, so that you can put it aside for a security deposit for a new apartment. You are so generous and loving to do that for your family, but maybe, for a season, it would be good to save that money for you and your daughter."

"That's true, Mr. Jack. I'm just nervous because I'm not sure if my family will understand. And they depend on my money."

I jumped in. "That is so hard, Darisa. I can't even imagine the burden it must be to provide for them, too. But I wonder if you had an honest conversation about your needs. Share with them that you and Anora are separated right now, but if you save the money you normally send them, you'll be able to get back together with her. And then, you can start sending them money again."

"Now that you can shower at our home, maybe you can cancel your gym membership, and that could save $30 each month. There are other ways you could save money, too. I know it's quick and easy to go through a drive-thru several times a day to get food and drinks, but we really would love for you to use the food we have here. It takes a little bit of planning, but at the end of a day, you could probably save twenty bucks or more on food, just by packing a lunch and bringing it with you," Jack suggested.

"Darisa, Jack and I aren't trying to tell you what to do, maybe just some things to consider, so that you could live with Anora again, sooner rather than later. Does that make sense?"

"Yeah, that does make sense. It's hard, but it's true. I love Anora and she needs to be living with me. And for that to happen, I do have to save money. I think I can do that."

"You're a strong woman, Darisa, who loves her daughter and we know you want to be the one tucking her in at night, and dropping her off at preschool each morning. We've seen how hard you work and we absolutely know you can do this. It will be difficult at first, but once you get used to bringing food with you, and once you have that hard conversation with your family, you'll be on your way to living with Anora again," Jack shared.

"You can do it, Darisa. We know you can!" I added.

It was there at the table where Jack and I helped cast a vision for what could be—Darisa and Anora together again. Darisa embraced the idea of spending less than she was making in order to save for her future, a future that would include living with her young daughter.

In about five months and with much effort, she saved enough money to find a small apartment to share with Anora. It was a blistering hot afternoon in late August when she turned the key in the lock of her new apartment door.

Darisa sent a text the first morning she walked Anora to preschool, just a few blocks from their new place. With lunch box in hand, and smiles a mile wide, Anora and Darisa beamed with joy in the attached selfie.

Mother and daughter were together once again. She had done it!

The following spring, they came to our United Nations

Easter (more on that in chapter nine), and Darisa was so proud to be living independently with her daughter. Over and over again, she thanked us for the help we offered. She shared that she was still making and taking a lunch with her when she worked, to save money to pay her bills, and also so she could send some to her family.

She called me Sister, and Jack Brother, and squeezed our kids as if they were her own. She now had family on this side of the ocean, too.

She belonged.

That Easter evening, after people packed up and headed out, Jack and I collapsed on the couch, exhausted in the very best of ways. Mixed with fatigue was the joy of seeing Darisa thrive. She and Anora were together again because of her hard work. All we provided was a cushion, some meals, and advice we had learned along the way. We saw a need, and we spontaneously decided to share our spare bedroom, some food, and kindness.

So why live this way?

Darisa's initial question—why would we let a stranger live with us—zeroes in on the upside-down nature of the Imperfect Welcome and begins to address the layers involved in living a life that leans toward radical hospitality.

So why live this way?

Was our effort to help Darisa worth it? Absolutely. There were certainly times we weren't so sure how her story would unfold because our stories don't always wrap up with a pretty little bow on a gift-wrapped box. And when the stories don't end with happily ever after, we are left with questions.

Do kindness and invitation into friendship even matter?

This world can be dark and lonely. That Easter evening, after reconnecting with Darisa and Anora, we realized the profound gift of welcome—of offering an invitation, whatever that might look like on any given day.

What about you? Do you, like me, see a lonely world filled with disconnected people? Maybe that lonely person looks radically different from you or, maybe, he or she could double as your twin. Perhaps you wonder if you could befriend a lonesome brother or sister who longs to connect. Or maybe, you're lonely and looking for connection, and in providing shelter for another weary, lost sojourner, you hope to find *your* place in this world.

Come join us.

We all need to belong.

02

Where in the World Am I?

"People will forget what you said.
They will forget what you did.
But they will never forget how you made them feel."

Maya Angelou

azing over the Rift Valley in November 1995, while visiting a friend who was teaching at Rift Valley Academy², an international school outside Nairobi, Kenya, Africa, I sensed that God was asking me this simple question: *"Would you do this for me? Would you give up your life in Chicago to go tell others how much I love them? About the Hope that I offer? About the Peace that I give?"*

My sincere and naïve answer? *"Of course, God. You know from the time I was little I have entertained thoughts of being a missionary. You put that desire in my heart. I'd totally do that for you!"*

That moment is so clear in my mind; it felt just shy of audible. I knew God was asking something of me.

But I was comfortable in Chicago and had made it my home. I was happily living the single, take-the-train, nine-to-five life. There was a guy I really liked, I was involved in my church, and I loved my friends. Life was good.

> Sometimes, devastation catapults us into life-changing experiences.

In what felt like a cruel turn of events, February rolled in and the guy I was crazy about took off.

Sometimes, devastation catapults us into life-changing experiences.

In August of 1996, at twenty-six years of age, I boarded a plane for the other side of the globe. I was mostly excited, but at some point, mid-flight, I realized I was alone. Tears streamed down my face as I thought back to the airport goodbyes. Three years is a long time to leave the ones you love.

Traveling to the other side of the earth was no joke. Three days. Layovers in various cities, and the longest in-air stretch was 15 hours from Hawaii to Southeast Asia. I arrived in Indonesia feeling disheveled at best.

Anticipation grew as my Air Garuda flight island-hopped across the Indonesian archipelago that mid-August evening. Every island landing was harrowing, and if Carrie Underwood's, "*Jesus Take the Wheel*" had been around back then, I would have bravely sung to my cabinmates.

Each take-off and landing brought me one island closer to a fresh start. I squinted through the blurry oval window during that final approach to Sentani International Airport, in the province of Irian Jaya (now called Papua). A rugged mountain with a breathtaking, cascading waterfall came into view, and I whispered to God in the quiet of seat 19A, "*Could that be my everyday view?*"

I was anxious and excited.

I didn't know a soul. An email had informed me that a man named Ken would pick me up at the airport. I had no idea what he looked like or where he was taking me, but I figured it would work itself out when I landed.

As it turns out, Ken was a local legend who oozes fun, so laughter settled into the van named The Green Machine as we zipped through town and up Pos 7 hill toward my new apartment.

When I saw the waterfall, I turned to Ken and said, "Is my apartment close?"

"Yep! About another quarter mile and we're there."

"Whoa! This is incredible."

Ken dropped me off with simple instructions: "Someone will take you to the pasar (market) later this morning. They'll teach you where to buy veggies and chicken and such. And then you'll go out for supper with several single teachers. Should be a fun night."

As he walked out the front door he also threw this little bit of happiness over his shoulder: "Oh, and by the way, there's no hot water. That's not really a thing around here, so boil water on the stove, and then ladle it from a bucket as your shower. The bucket's in the bathroom."

"Well, that doesn't seem easy."

Chuckling to himself, the screen door closed and there I was, all alone.

At five thirty that evening, I was whisked to the home of strangers for supper. Barreling down the mountain, the distant sky was filled with brilliant pinks, rich burnt oranges, and show-stopping purples overlaid on endless clouds of all shapes and sizes. That was the first of countless sunsets I would watch over the following three years.

Sunsets on the equator *never* got old.

As was the custom, new arrivals in town were treated to home-cooked meals their first few weeks. I vividly remember so much about that night—the white-tiled floors and screened, louvered windows, replete with security bars. Stifling hot equatorial air punched me in the gut as I glanced sideways at the long table set with rice, veggies, and chicken. No doubt, the chicken had been free range just a few hours prior.

It was simple and inviting. Those around the table welcomed me in, and in my exhaustion, I pushed to stay awake in spite of jet-lag.

"Where are you from, Alysa? What will you be doing here in Sentani? How long will you stay?"

"Well, I'm Canadian, but I live in Chicago, well, *lived* in Chicago, and I'm here to teach Language Arts to the sixth, seventh, and eighth graders up at Hillcrest. I'll be here for three years."[3]

An exchange of information, alongside friendly banter, made a smooth entry into Indonesia. They were an easy crowd, willing to include me, the stranger, into their circle.

Mid-meal, a lizard dropped from the ceiling—right onto the table. Somehow it missed the bowl of rice, thank you very much. I screamed, it scurried, and my new friends howled as the conversation continued.

An actual animal landed on the table, and no one seemed to care.

Where in the world am I?

This continued throughout the meal, where I would spot a lizard scampering up the living room wall and out an impossibly tiny slit in the window screen. The next one would pop out from under a door and zip toward the kitchen.

They all seemed oblivious.

My heart thudded and my curiosity crept out much like the lizard that suddenly appeared next to my rice.

"So. I see we've got lizards. Tell me what sort of snakes we're working with! Deadly? Gigantic? Poisonous but you wouldn't die if it bit you? Do you ever see them in your house or is it only when you're out hiking the jungle trails?

I don't really know any of you, but please lie. Just tell me you've never seen one."

Insert guffaws.

"Can't really lie," she said. "They're around. Various kinds. Watch out for the death adders, and the really bright snakes. *A snake with death in its name?* The brighter, the deadlier. *Deadly?* Sometimes you'll see snakes slithering in your yard and other times, they'll be dead, stretched out across the road. The snakes on the road are there because the nationals want whomever drives over it to receive the evil spirits from the snake—a transfer of evil belief."

"Here's the best advice we could give? Occasionally you'll see them around your toilet bowl, so make sure to check the bottom of the toilet *before* you sit down, *especially* in the middle of the night. They love the cool of the bowl," he said as they all howled at my dismay.

"OH COME OFF IT. I can't do this. I hate snakes."

"We've got lots of big spiders, too," one of them joked.

"I'm not sure I like you anymore. Can you please pass the rice?"

Laughter filled the air.

"Okay, how about this? Tell me about the ocean. I love oceans. They're lovely, and blue, and I'm assuming warm since we're on the equator. Is there one within driving distance?"

Mid-sentence the lights went out, the town generators ceased, and we were sitting in pitch darkness. Again, this did not phase *anyone* around the table. Conversation continued as if they didn't even realize we were sitting in the dark. I couldn't see my hand in front of my face (I do not exaggerate), and no one was concerned. No, not one. In time, the host casually found and lit a candle, as if as an afterthought.

Oh my word! Where am I?

Now, many years removed, I often return to my thoughts about that first night in Indonesia. Little did I know that within a few short weeks, I, too, would be unphased by lizards roaming my home and power outages that lasted for hours. It is remarkable how we acclimate to new surroundings. I belonged to this ragtag bunch of adventurous souls who were *just* crazy enough to abandon all they had ever known to traipse to an unknown, unfamiliar land.

What began as a dodgy first night in Irian Jaya (hailed one of the most primitive places on earth), over time became to me, a splendid glimpse of heaven. This was a place where strangers far from their passport countries were thrust together, and in order to survive, welcoming others in was a better alternative than going it alone. So, here we were, dozens of people living imperfectly, figuring things out as we went along, surviving because we were doing it together.

Welcome was a way of life, almost as if survival depended on it. Which I'd argue, it did.

Here on Earth, I call this the Imperfect Welcome.

There in Irian Jaya, none of us had extended family, so we all became each other's. Welcome was a way of life, almost as if survival depended on it. Which, I'd argue, it did. Strangers didn't stay strangers for long and within days I was in relationships that, decades later, are still some of my favorites of all.

Sentani in the 1990s had zero fancy homes, welcome mats, or matching dishes. There were no leather recliners or cable television stations. Red meat and cheese at the local grocery store? Forget about it; you're looking at a trip to Australia for that goodness. By normal North American standards, there were few comforts and conveniences. Yet the welcome I experienced in that community superseded any comfort that could be bought by material goods. There was a sense of "as it was intended to be," in shared meals with acquaintances turned friends, laughter over our latest slip-ups in a foreign land, and time spent visiting in a culture that valued relationship over productivity.

To welcome was a gift.

My first six months I was invited into the Stuber world and almost nightly, Roger, Gwen, and their kids saved a spot for me and other single missionaries around their table. It is worth noting that they were not living in luxury and did not have heaps of extra food in their cupboards. Gwen was able to take the scarcest of ingredients, produce simple yet delicious meals, and share with a spirit of generosity. Not once do I remember feeling as if I was putting them out by being another mouth to feed. It never occurred to me how presumptuous it was to show up at their house for supper so regularly, but as I was settling in without my family nearby, I needed to belong.

Early on, I claimed my place in their family, and in the evenings once dishes were done, we sat together and read, often by candlelight because of the whole sporadic electricity situation. We laughed over the kids' antics at school, and we sometimes played a raucous game of Dutch Blitz, all while being entertained by Roger's harrowing stories of life as a jungle pilot.

What a gift, right? They lived an undecorated life that communicated, "Come on in and join us. Can you set the table? And could you babysit the kids next week when we go into Jayapura for fingerprinting and visa requirements? And do you want to go with us into the Highlands for Christmas vacation?"

My life was transformed in Indonesia, initially by the Stubers, and then by the Dukes, Isaacs, Hans, Wileys, Maxeys, Wilsons, and Johnsens, among many others. I had no way of knowing that the gift of belonging I received in Indonesia would shape who I am today and how I would want to live moving forward.

As I stepped into the families I met in Indonesia, I became friend, sister, and auntie. Whether it was cutting pineapple for Friday night pizza, standing in the kitchen trading life stories, playing cards after supper, or eating popcorn while watching movies, by sharing their lives these precious friends modeled the Imperfect Welcome.

Theirs was an open-handed posture. They wanted me there with them, and that felt so good. I was included and I can't think of a much better gift than that.

To be sure, there was a cost involved for these families who invited me in: there was a financial cost; a cost of time and energy to let me step into their homes so regularly; and there was the inconvenience at the end of the evening, when either the husband or one of the teen-age sons had to follow me as I drove my moped back to my home a few kilometers away, to make sure I arrived safely. There had been too many encounters with drunk men, so it simply wasn't wise for me to drive alone after dark.

As a wildly idealistic "I'm going to change the world" romantic, I thought God would "use me" to do amazing things for him. I mean, I was willing to go to the ends of the Earth, for Pete's sake. You name the cliché, I was there for it!

But from 1996-1999, on jungle hikes and tropical beaches, around dining room tables and on living room sofas, I received the benefit of those who counted the cost and chose to invite me in. I learned where true change happens. It happens, as Psalm 68:6 says, when "God places the lonely in families." It happens in the belonging together, when strangers become friends, then family.

My husband, Jack, had his own journey toward hospitality. Jeff and Ramona Tucker, church friends a little older than he, modeled for him a "come on in" way of living. Right out of high school, Jack found himself at their home on more days than he could count. He would show up unannounced (conveniently around suppertime), and Ramona would fold him into the chores of setting the table or stirring the soup. He was learning the art of hospitality and she made it seem natural; it's just what they did.

My journey looked different from Jack's, and yours will look different from ours.

Those tiny, faithful pebbles that others dropped into the waters of my experiences in Indonesia have, decades later, made their way across the Pacific, swelling over the miles, turning into waves that lap the shores of Lake Michigan with a consistent, life-giving joy that brings purpose to my days. Many of my former students who return to the U.S. have passed through our front door and back into our hearts when we occasionally host them in our Chicago home. To some degree, I have been able to reciprocate the hospitality shown to me by their parents.

Jack came to visit me in Indonesia and one experience he had there still affects him today. The Wiley house was Sentani's equivalent of New York's Grand Central Station. Joan Wiley was, and still is, a teacher at the international school where I taught, and I became dear friends with her and her family. During Jack's stay, we stopped over for supper and a visit at Joan and Wally's home. Joan walked in after a long, particularly humid day of teaching on the equator.

While her house was usually full of kids, that day it was

packed—maybe because the kids were hanging out with this mysterious Jack "friend" of Aunt Alysa's who had traveled all the way from the United States for a visit.

Joan shed her black, oversized bag by the front door, added her shoes to the pile of flip-flops, stopped at the table to help one of the kids with a homework question, and made straight for the kitchen. At one point she asked for a headcount for supper.

Jack followed her into the kitchen, and asked if he could help.

"Sure," she said. "Why don't you start setting the table while I pull out the veggies."

"Joan, you've gotta be exhausted. You've worked since early this morning, you have a pile of dishes that need to be washed, you're feeding who knows how many people, and you just helped someone with homework."

She paused, then said something he will always remember, "Jack, serving others will cost you something. But you don't get the joy from serving others unless you accept the cost along with it."

There is a cost in serving, and in our twenties, before meeting and marrying, Jack and I did not know much about the cost, nor did we have vision statements outlining key strategies for effective, meaningful interaction with strangers. We weren't that intentional. Our hospitable hearts evolved over time through new experiences as we shared our lives with others.

At the time, the families who had invited us in had no

idea that their lifestyle of welcome imprinted something inside each of us that said, "This is a meaningful way to live."

You might be wondering what all this has to do with you.

Well, we each get 60, 70, maybe 80 years on planet Earth, and what we do with those years actually matters. The small choices we make each day ripple onto others. We don't always see the effects of our choices, as our immediate circle of friends and acquaintances change over the years, but beneath the surface of what we do—jobs, hobbies, church, life-maintenance activities—we find our "how."

In our younger years, when Jack and I connected with more mature people, we were shown how to create an environment of belonging. And because of regular efforts to include us, Jack and I learned the value and gift of including others into our lives.

How can you and I adopt the Imperfect Welcome as a lifestyle?

Maybe we start small, but we do it regularly. My current bent toward welcome is the result of one tiny stone after another thrown into the waters of my life over the decades. What started as that little voice whispering, "Wow, this feels good to be included," is now a mantra on the welcome mat at our front door and the walls of our living room: "Come As You Are" because "You Are Welcome Here."

An invitation of welcome can indeed come with a cost,

which varies in each individual circumstance, but we have found that the connection is usually worth the associated cost. In 2009, we said yes to Afghani refugees, and while the cost was extensive, the connection was priceless.

03

Do You Want to
Hold My Hand?

*"Christian hospitality cannot be domesticated or
managed; it takes us on an adventure ...
that can be truly remarkable."*

Elizabeth Newman

I t was 2007. Fatima, her eight-month old son, Abdul,
and her husband Jamil, fled Kabul, Afghanistan, for the
Pakistani border. Jamil's connection to the foreign mili-
tary had put his life in danger.

As their vehicle approached the TorKham border,
tension mounted and they were unsure if they would be
allowed to cross. Fatima glanced at her tiny child between

them, and then to her husband, with mounting fear. The Pakistani Border Control began their questioning.

"You, get out! Stand over here. With the baby, too," the guard boomed as he leaned into the car, directing his attention at the mother and son.

In shock, Fatima quietly gathered up their son and did as she was told. They stood a few meters away and watched as the situation escalated; the guard yelled at Jamil, who was sitting in the driver's seat of their black sedan, while he attempted to secure entry into Pakistan.

Showing no mercy, the guard turned and said, "The woman and child can enter, but you must return. Say your goodbyes," he shouted.

"We will go back with you, Jamil, and return together another day. Please. I don't want to go without you. PLEASE, we should stay together," Fatima pleaded.

"No, my Love. You go on to safety now. You have the phone number for Layla. She will arrange transport for you to be taken to Islamabad and I will be back soon," Jamil assured his wife.

"Please, Jamil. Please. Don't leave us," Fatima wept as she clung to their son, Abdul.

"I'll join you in a few days, Love. I promise." These were his parting words as he rolled up the window, backed up the car, and turned toward Afghanistan's capital.

He never returned.

He was murdered on the road back to Kabul.

Fatima lived in Pakistan as a widow and single mom,

spent most days in her small apartment, and attempted to make herself invisible when she came and went. With no work visa, her days consisted of part-time work in an office (with Abdul asleep under her desk), meetings at the United Nations (UN) office trying to secure safe passage to a new country, and occasional trips to the neighborhood grocery store.

Fatima received little money for the work she did, so by the time she paid her monthly rent and utility bills, only a tiny amount remained for food. Days melted together and fear gripped her mind, leaving her unable to sleep and concentrate. She passed the time looking out the tiny front window of her apartment as she longed for home, as one might long for fresh water in the Sahara Desert.

Eventually, through a rigorous, two-year process, she was given refugee status through the UN. She was starting over as American Airlines Flight #334 touched down in Chicago, Illinois, USA, on November 4th, 2009.

Wednesday afternoon, November 4th

That same afternoon, inside Terminal Three of O'Hare International Airport, my kids and I stood at the base of the escalator, waiting for strangers. We knew we were look-ing for an Afghani mom named Fatima and her young son named Abdul. That's all we knew.

Because we arrived ridiculously early, the area was empty, but I noticed an elderly woman lingering nearby. We had been told there might be a woman there because the refugee mother we were to meet had one connection in the United States. And it was here in Chicago.

In time I scooted close and said, "Ma'am, by chance you wouldn't be waiting for a mother and her son from Afghanistan, would you?"

"Yes, I am."

"Oh, us, too! I'm Alysa and this is Maddie and Jackson. We are volunteers with World Relief,[4] and we're here to welcome them to Chicago and bring them to their apartment."

"So nice. My name is Layla. I am...how do you say... like an aunt?"

We stood and made small talk, each looking at the escalator as if willing them to appear, while Jackson rolled around on the floor and Maddie lay beside him (we raised them right!), intermittently asking, "How much longer, Mom?"

Come to find out, Layla was a close family friend who also had made her way to Pakistan and then to the U.S. as a refugee, months prior. Early in our conversation it was apparent that her transition had been lonely and difficult.

She looked away, choked up a bit, and said, "I'm probably going to cry when I see Abdul."

Without much thought I asked the stupidest question. "Have you been lonely in Chicago?"

"So lonely." Tears flooded as she excused herself.

In that moment, we gathered Layla into our family.

As we waited, Maddie asked, "What happened to

Abdul's daddy?" Layla looked at me with hesitation and a saddened disposition. She paused, then quietly shared, "He was killed."

Through tears I explained to Maddie that there were bad men in the country they were from that did bad things, and Abdul's daddy died. The whole time I was trying to simplify this explanation, Layla nodded her head in agreement.

I turned to her and said, "I am so, so, sorry. We really have no idea the suffering you and your family have gone through."

With a quiet voice and misty eyes, she replied, "You are right. You have no idea."

Silence ensued, both of us lost in our own thoughts. My mind flitted through our family's journey that had led us to American Airlines' baggage claim that day. We had prayed and hoped for this moment and said yes to being a "Good Neighbor" months prior, but did not know the people we were saying yes to.

They should be here soon. And then what? I hope that somehow we can help this mom and son not feel quite so alone. I can't even imagine how they must feel right now. Starting over, in a foreign country, without their husband and daddy.

Somehow, this section of the airport seemed quieter than normal, but after an hour or so, movement at the top of the escalator caught my eye. Traveler after traveler jostled into position and streamed down the thin conveyor belt, purses and backpacks slung over shoulders, weary faces focused on finding the carousel that contained their luggage. We were curious; could this be their flight?

Dozens of people came and went, and the crowd thinned back down to an occasional trickle, a trickle so thin we wondered: *Did they make it through customs in Atlanta? Did they miss their flight? Where could they be?*

And then—in a moment I will never forget—a woman in an oversized, pale-green men's long-sleeved shirt, carrying a plastic shopping bag, stepped into view at the top of the escalator, with a sweet, dark-haired, dark-eyed young son, carrying a stuffed animal equal his size. In what felt like slow-motion, Layla moved toward the bottom of the escalator with her smile widening as mother and son came nearer.

The little boy stepped onto solid ground, let go of his mother's hand, and as he ran toward Layla, she squatted on one knee and scooped him into the most tender hug I have ever witnessed. Quiet words spilled out of Layla as she buried her head in Abdul's little neck, while tears of loneliness escaped her eyes. In time, she stood and hugged Fatima, each with a relieved smile that communicated safety and comfort in a family member's arms.

We let them have their moment and eventually stepped into the scene.

Looking at both Layla and Fatima, trying to recover from the moving experience I had just witnessed, I launched into an awkward introduction. "Well, hi, ummm, my name is Alysa. And this is my daughter Maddie, and this is my son Jackson. We are so excited to meet you. May we help you with your things? We have a car and we can take you to your apartment if you would like. We are so happy you have arrived."

Layla, knowing a fair bit of English, translated into Pashto for Fatima, who softly smiled and said, "*Dera manana*. Thank you. Yes."

In that moment Maddie walked over to Abdul, bent down eye-to-eye and said in a quiet voice, "You're safe now. Do you want to hold my hand?"

Three-year-old Abdul did not know one word of English, but somehow, Maddie's five-year-old outstretched hand and hushed words, offered alongside a warm smile and gentle posture set him at ease. In return, Abdul clasped Maddie's hand and, eventually Jackson's, too. For the next twenty minutes the three navigated O'Hare International Airport as new friends.

That day was as sacred as communion in church, and has become a day we recall yearly. A mysterious exchange of hope happened in the offering and the accepting of welcome and kindness. It was just an ordinary Wednesday afternoon that would forever mark our lives.

A mysterious exchange of hope happened in the offering and the accepting of welcome and kindness.

What we didn't know then is that this initial welcome

would grow into imperfect strangers who became imperfect friends, who eventually became imperfect family.

———

How did it start?

Jack and I were each serving in different roles at our local church and other parachurch organizations, yet we wanted to serve as a family. Jack visited Chicago's Cook County Jail most Friday nights, encouraging the incarcerated. As a stay-at-home mom, I taught and led women's and moms' groups, as well as chased down service opportunities that excited our then five-year-old daughter. In any given month we visited homeless shelters, packed food to address global starvation, or dropped off coffee during the frigid winter days for our local *Chicago Tribune* man who sold papers on a busy street corner near our home.

February through October (2009)

We knew it was time to walk intentionally toward a common goal of serving together, but didn't know exactly what that would involve, so we started by noticing which stories sparked curiosity. Sometimes that meant the narrative in Chicago, and other times the global news challenged us. The common thread for both Jack and me was usually a longing to befriend those in dire need. Those pushed to the fringes of society.

We started asking questions such as: "What need could

we address as a family?" and, "What makes sense in this chapter of our lives with little kids?"

During that season we became aware of World Relief, an organization that dedicates time and resources to helping refugees and immigrants rebuild their lives once they leave their home countries and land on U.S. soil. World Relief piqued our interest, so we attended an informational meeting hosted at our church.

We were in deep with littles at that time—Maddie, five, and Jackson, two—and as I sat in that meeting and heard the stories and saw the images of women running for their lives, carrying their children on their backs and in their arms, seeing fear and desperation in their eyes, knowing they might arrive in the United States all alone, something inside me broke. I knew I had to do something. I might not be a doctor who could offer medical help, or a lawyer who could offer legal assistance, but I could be a friend.

As you might guess, we signed up to host a family; we offered to be, in their terms, a "Good Neighbor." It was time. We felt the desire to serve so we took another step that seemed right to us, not truly knowing what our yes would mean and how it would impact us.

The Good Samaritan in Luke chapter 10 is often cited—as it should be—in the context of radical welcome.[5] This is where World Relief gets their term Good Neighbor. The crux of the story? The Samaritan man was on a business trip and took notice of a man left for dead on the other side of the road, whom others had passed by and ignored.

The Samaritan neighbor gave dignity to the injured man by noticing, helping, and providing health care.

What is often overlooked is the fact that not only did the Samaritan man do the right thing in the moment—help a guy in need—he also crossed significant racial and ethnic divides, putting his own safety and reputation at risk, to meet the needs of a stranger. These two men were as different as water and oil; they were enemies in the world's eyes. The Samaritan man went where his culture said he shouldn't go, and he put fears, excuses, and personal inconveniences aside, simply to show kindness. Did he analyze the risk and evaluate his schedule to see if he could squeeze this interruption into his busy day? Nah. He just did it. He might have been afraid—the story doesn't say—but he moved *toward* someone radically different than himself. He did the right thing without regard to consequence.

And while the parable is short, I'd venture to say that if Jesus had shared details of the Samaritan's entire life, we might see that his was a *life of welcome* that started well before Luke 10 unfolded. Being faithful to welcome in the smaller circumstances helps bigger opportunities feel less risky.

We had no idea what we were getting into, but we felt a sense of calm mingled with excitement. We learned World Relief's minimum requirements to come alongside a refugee family, and we said, "Okay, that's doable." It boiled down to setting up their apartment prior to their arrival, greeting them at the airport, bringing them to their apartment, and meeting with them once a week for a few months.

We could do that.

We took lots of small steps in an intentional direction—the direction to serve as a family—and becoming a Good Neighbor was yet another small step in our journey. We couldn't have jumped from our February hearts that said, "Let's serve together as a family," to our November hearts that said, "Let's spend several days a week helping a refugee family," in one fell swoop. If I could take a guess, I'd say that would have been an overwhelming leap, one we wouldn't have been willing to take. The cost of the commitment became feasible because of the bite-sized nature of the journey.

The cost of the commitment became feasible because of the bite-sized nature of the journey.

Over the months leading up to the new family's arrival, we collected items at garage sales using a list provided by World Relief as our guide. When we were out and about as a family, if we spotted a garage sale sign, we'd zip over to the curb, jump out with our list in hand, and let the fun begin.

"There's a sign, Dad!" Maddie piped up from the back seat.

It was the best kind of treasure hunt with four sets of

eyes looking to stock our refugees' home with items both practical and pretty.

I remember one particular garage sale. We pulled over, got out of the car, and walked toward the apartment building courtyard. We instantly knew we had hit the motherload, as there were piles of kitchen items on a blanket.

"Wow, you're gathering up a lot of things for a kitchen. Did you just move here?" asked the homeowner.

"No. Actually, we're pulling things together to help a refugee family. We don't know them yet, but we're collecting things so that when we get the call that they have arrived in Chicago, we can set up their apartment," Jack shared as the kids schlepped the last of the items over to the table.

"Wow. That's so neat. I'll tell you what. I'll give all of this to you for five bucks. It's a small thing I can do to help, too. Sound good?"

There on that sidewalk, with grateful hearts, we promised to share their story of kindness to a family they had never met.

Monday afternoon, November 2nd

World Relief called saying a refugee family of two (a mother and son) would be arriving on Wednesday, just a day and a half later. Would we like to be their Good Neighbor?

By late Monday evening, after discussion and prayer, we said, "Yes!"

Tuesday morning, November 3rd

Maddie and I drove to World Relief to pick up the keys to their apartment. I could barely see Maddie in her car seat because our car was crammed tight with pots and pans, sheets and blankets, lamps and side tables, and accoutrements of various shapes, sizes, and functions, all things necessary to turn a blank canvas into a warm, livable space.

We arrived at their apartment building; the long, dark hall that led to their door looked a bit foreboding, but we started hauling things in just the same. We piled load after load onto the queen-size bed frame and mattress that had been delivered by World Relief.

We spent the rest of that day cleaning, organizing, and setting up their apartment. One of my favorite memories is of five-year-old Maddie making the large closet into the three-year-old son's bedroom. The stuffed animals were placed just so. The little lamp was situated on the tiny bedside table and books were left for easy discovery. Maddie worked tirelessly to welcome our new friends to Chicago.

We were curious. Who would this family be and how would we communicate with them if they didn't know English? We asked the question that we regularly seemed to ask: What have we gotten ourselves into this time?

Wednesday afternoon, November 4th

After collecting their bags, we left the airport together, with Fatima and the three kids squeezed into the back seat of our Chevy Malibu, while Layla, who knew more English, sat up front with me. We inched our way toward Chicago's North Side, mere blocks from Lake Michigan. Their new community, Rogers Park, was home to countless immigrants from dozens of countries, and was one of Chicago's most diverse zip codes. Devon Avenue is exciting and busy with cultures colliding at every street corner. As we drove through, I couldn't help but wonder what Fatima was thinking about. *Did the newness accentuate the ache in her heart for home? Or did this feel comforting to her in some way?*

We had one important pit stop to make—take-out for supper. We toyed with the idea of dazzling them with Lou Malnati's[6] deep-dish pizza (as one does when one entertains visitors in our hometown), but in the end, we thought offering food tasting similar to home might be a gentler, more comforting entry into their new, strange world.

I remember thinking, *"They're actually here. We are finally meeting our family."* The dream that took root in February was unfolding. We each had to walk our own journey to get to this point, taking steps that led us to this moment in Chicago's rush hour traffic. What we didn't know then was that this would be the first of hundreds of 30-minute, one-way trips from our home to theirs, that we would make over the coming years.

We were just an ordinary family, three strangers, and some radical hospitality colliding.

Jack met us at their apartment and with all the

appropriate pleasantries and introductions, we walked into their new home together. Maddie confidently led Abdul and our son Jackson to Abdul's own little space and before long, they were scooched together on the bed, piled high with stuffed animals, as Maddie read a book to the younger boys. Remember, Abdul did not know a single word of English, but there they sat. Kids being kids.

We showed Fatima around her new home, filled with items new and used, many from garage sales that we and our friends had collected over the months. It was a slow process because each time she opened a drawer or a door she would pause and exclaim, "Wow!" repeatedly. When she opened the fridge and found chicken and veggies, Coco-Cola and milk, she was especially delighted.

She was genuinely grateful and appreciative and at one point turned and said (through Layla's translation), "And you don't even know me!"

I couldn't hold them in. Tears slid down my face and Fatima reached over, gave me a hug, took my face in her hands, and wiped my tears. "Oh, no cry."

Turning to Layla I said, "Oh, these are happy tears," and with quite a lengthy discussion, she was able to translate the concept of such a thing into Pashto for Fatima.

"Oh, good, good," she sighed. "Happy tears."

I shared with Layla, who shared with Fatima, that she was such a strong woman for all she had gone through. She glanced at Abdul, pointed, and with an air of determination said, "I do it for him!"

That evening I lost count of the number of times she exclaimed, "You did this for us, and you did not know us! Wow. Too nice. Too nice. *Dera manana*."

There is a mysterious—I'd call it divine—exchange that happens when strangers connect through acts of kindness, and this mysterious interchange is beneficial for both. God says the two things he cares most about are 1) that we love him with every part of who we are, and 2) that we love our neighbors as ourselves.[7] When one person chooses to step toward a neighbor, Jesus says it is as if that act of kindness (inviting a stranger in, feeding the hungry, clothing the naked, etc.), is actually being offered to Jesus himself. He identifies with those on the edges of our societies and longs for us to step toward them because in stepping toward strangers, we actually step into his presence.

I need to chew on that for a minute. We meet God in new ways when we step into relationship with strangers? Hmmm.

We were strangers thrown together by a phone call and a plane's arrival on a certain date in a certain city. And it was in the stepping toward each other where we each stepped toward God. I'll never forget Fatima's repeated words, "You did this for us and you did not know us." Jesus was on to something when he said, "…I was a stranger and you invited me in…"[8]

The Imperfect Welcome alleviates the ache of loneliness we all occasionally experience. Want to give it a try?

04

Brownies, A Winter Coat, and a House Full of Sisters

"No act of kindness is ever wasted."

Aesop

Within days of our meeting, Fatima began sharing bits of her story. She had attended university where she learned some English, so we hobbled along using her limited English, hand motions, sounds, guesses, and Google.

"Do you mean car? Vroom vroom?" I would ask.

"No. Meow. Meow."

'Oh, cat. C. A. T. Cat." I would slowly spell out the

words and little by little, her vocabulary exploded those first several months.

Often our time was filled with laughter, but periodically her eyes looked lifeless as she stared through us, lost in a memory. With tears we listened, full of sorrow for her losses and the suffering she had faced.

"Fatima, it is good for us to hear your story because we cannot imagine what you went through. We don't really know what life is like in much of the world," I said one afternoon in the quiet of our basement.

"Alysa, I was so scared—too scared. The Taliban makes me fearful."

My original blog came on the scene in 2007, as a place to store my thoughts, photos, and family stories. Before long hundreds of people were following our family's daily journey. I didn't know that Facebook and my blog, both relatively new concepts to me in the mid-2000s, would be instrumental in bringing friends around the globe along on our journey with Fatima and Abdul.

During the initial season of their arrival, I blogged almost daily about our new friendship. People quickly fell in love with them, wanting to hear more, as if it were a bedtime story we all want our parents to keep telling. *"And then what? Just one more story. Please?!"*

I straddled the fine line of sharing our mutual story of connection, while also wanting to protect their privacy and honor their story. Readers followed along, and with Fatima's blessing and permission, I shared photos and snippets of their story. I knew if I could share my family's story of connection with Fatima and Abdul, with those who knew and trusted me, it might compel others to reach out in a spirit of welcome, too.

I found myself surprised by the joy and satisfaction I was experiencing in being in close relationship with Fatima. We belly-laughed over our commonalities *and* the things we did and said that were wildly different. Did you know that they sing "Happy Birthday" in English at birthday parties in Afghanistan? Who knew?

I was learning to see life through a Central Asian lens in conjunction with my Western lens, and vice versa for her. We had a cross-cultural experience, and I was there for it! Was I helping her, or was she helping me? To this day, I would argue it was split right down the middle.

As the world was becoming aware of the global refugee crisis, Jack, Maddie, Jackson, and I were rubbing shoulders with a family who had lived that reality. Our connection became a connection for our Western friends and family.

Welcome is contagious.

Fatima and Abdul became virtual friends to scores of people and their story compelled others to action. What started out as offers to donate warm clothes or purchase things as needed, quickly became requests to actually meet them.

Welcome is contagious.

That first night in their new home, I shared with Fatima that it wasn't just our family that had furnished their apartment. We had a lot of church friends and family who had donated money and items to help. She immediately said, "I like meet them."

Here's how that unfolded.

Tuesday morning, November 10th

Jennifer opened her laptop and read the email I sent out early that morning:

> Hey friends, I know it's super short notice, but Fatima, Abdul, and Layla are spending the day at our home on Thursday, and I'm thinking of having a 'come-and-go' all day. If you're available and want to pop over for a visit we'd love that. I'll have snacks and an easy lunch so just come whenever it works in your schedule. I can't wait for you to meet them. You're gonna fall in love! Love, Alysa

Jennifer had been following the story on my blog, and with flexibility in her schedule she decided she would come. She gathered her sons, Raymond and Jonathan, told them a bit about Abdul and his mother, Fatima, and then spent the afternoon picking out clothes to share from her boys' closet.

Wednesday evening, November 11th

I set the new coat on our couch that Angie had dropped off earlier that afternoon and could hardly wait to give it to Layla the following day.

The story behind that coat was something divine.

This was to be Layla's first winter in Chicago and I learned that she worked the late shift at Walmart, far from her apartment, often waiting thirty to forty-five minutes to catch the bus in the frigid midnight air. Her current jacket situation was what most would call a light fall coat, and it was not going to work come January.

For all the drawbacks of social media, there are upsides. After learning of her need for proper winter attire, I called on my Facebook friends.

"Anyone have a warm women's winter coat they could donate for someone in great need? Probably a size large."

The response came within minutes.

"I have one that I'd LOVE to give her and wait 'til you hear the whole story. God is AMAZING." *(emphasis hers)*

Angie shared that earlier that autumn she'd had a garage sale where she tried to sell an expensive, brand new, down-filled, winter coat she had purchased off-season for her sister—a coat her sister didn't want. Angie had missed the deadline to return it to Marshall Field & Co., so it landed in the garage sale pile. She had tagged it with a reasonable price but not typical "garage sale low," hoping to recover some of the money she had originally spent. Surely someone would sense the incredible deal and snatch it up as winter quickly approached.

Nearing the end of that day, a young woman relentlessly haggled for the coat. Maybe she assumed Angie wouldn't want to bring it back into her home; that she'd take a buck or two and be done with it.

"Sorry, ma'am. I can't sell it for that cheap. I'd rather give the coat to someone who actually needs it than sell it for next to nothing."

She couldn't bear to part with the coat at the garage sale and felt in her spirit that she wasn't to sell it because somewhere there was a specific need for it.

She tucked it away, waiting for the right moment. And then she saw my ask on social media.

This woman—a stranger to her—was to be the new owner of that coat.

Thursday early morning, November 12th

Just eight days after their arrival, I set snacks on the table, pulled out the brownie box mix, and sat for a few minutes before driving to pick up Fatima, Abdul, and Layla. In the quiet of the morning, I thought that it was going to be so fun to share them with others. The gift they had become to us would be passed along to my friends.

Others were joining because we all wanted to help and learn. Most of us knew the Afghanistan narrative through sound bites on the news, so now that we were friends with a family from that region, we could learn what life was really like and we could begin to imagine ourselves in their shoes. And as we learned, we grew.

The Imperfect Welcome fuels compassion.

Thursday mid-morning, November 12th

Our home was electric as the doorbell rang continuously; friends came and went, offering the warmest of welcomes to our new Afghani family.

Cynthia was among the first to visit. When I emailed her about coming and bringing her boys, Ethan (5) and Edward (3), to meet Abdul, hers was an immediate and excited "Yes!"

As they were leaving their house that morning, Cynthia noticed that Ethan had on his coat and hat and was also holding his new Tonka truck in his arms.

That's when it dawned on Cynthia. Ethan wanted to give his favorite truck to Abdul.

"Ethan, that's so kind! I know you want to give our new friend something super special, but what if you gave him your old truck instead of your new one? It's cool, too. It looks great and I think he would love it. Or, you could pick out a totally different toy for him?"

Ethan was insistent that he wanted to give *this* truck to Abdul.

"You know that whatever you give, you won't get back, right?" Cynthia warned.

"I know, Mom."

And that was that.

They arrived at the door and Ethan carried his Tonka truck inside and passed it over to Abdul, who was nestled close to his mother.

Abdul tentatively held it while Fatima exclaimed, "Wow, Abdul, look. This is too nice. Oh, *dera manana*. Thank you."

The heart of a child will always blow my mind and move me to tears. Ethan got it. He wasn't coerced into giving his best. He gave his prized possession with joy, open hands, and a generous attitude, and whether he knew it or not, he was "cheerfully giving,"[9] and "practicing hospitality."[10]

If we'll let them, our children—like Ethan—can lead us straight to God's heart for orphans and widows and others in need. A straight shot to the core of radical hospitality.

I'm quite certain there is no mention of a Tonka truck in the Bible, but I know that in that moment we were standing on holy ground, watching a generous, costly love offering exchange hands between two young boys.

Jennifer and her boys arrived next, itching to meet Fatima and Abdul. After introductions, Raymond and Jonathan scooted a huge bag of clothing toward Abdul.

Excitedly, Fatima said, "Wow. This is too nice. WOW. *Dera manana!*" (*emphasis hers*)

Fatima's immediate response was to pull Jennifer—still a stranger at this point—into an embrace, kissing as she toggled from cheek to cheek.

When Fatima stepped off the plane, her earthly possessions fit into two large suitcases. What little clothing she had would not support her for the winter, so the overstuffed bag of hand-me-down clothing from Jennifer communicated a mutual understanding from one mom to another.

At the core of what moms want for our children is that basic needs be met: safety, shelter, clothing, and food. And somewhere deep within, we hope they will have lives that thrive. The clothes in that bag were not new, and they weren't offered from a place of pity. They were offered because one mom knew what she would need if the tables were turned.

It was in the shared space of my small kitchen that the currency of connection was passed from hand to hand.

While we had only known her eight days at this point, the open house marked a shift in Fatima's fragile spirit. In the middle of snatching bits and pieces of conversation, just a gaggle of women being women, she found familiarity. It was in that house full of chatting women, dishes clanging, and children bouncing around the lower level like ping pong balls across the table, that Fatima experienced a small taste of home. It was in the stirring of ingredients and the preparing of food that a bond was forged.

What Fatima *actually* needed?

Sisters.

When Fatima left Afghanistan, she said goodbye to her mother and five sisters along with a culture that places high value on communal living. For her, a house full of women was salve for her wounded soul. It was in the shared space of my small kitchen that the currency of connection was passed from hand to hand.

That day we howled as we taught Fatima to use a hand mixer—making brownies from a box. Who knew a small handheld kitchen appliance could bring such wonder? She marveled at the speed and ease of the process and could hardly wait for those brownies to be done, standing guard over the oven door the entire time they baked. Every minute or two she would bend over and peek through the oven glass to note the progress. Apparently, they love chocolate in Afghanistan, too!

Abdul was guarded, and yet that day he skipped through our home, joining in games of chase and stuffed animals, learning new English words, and most importantly, he was just a kid being a kid with other kids.

At the end of the day, after the last of our friends closed the door, we rested in our front room with cheeks that hurt from smiling, and throats that were just a wee bit hoarse from hours of chatter. As contentment spread across her face, Fatima turned and said, "I like them. Your friends are too nice. Too, too nice!"

That first Christmas, our family was headed to Canada but because of their refugee status, Fatima and Abdul could not leave the country with us.

I couldn't bear the thought of their being alone for two weeks. In those days, we really were their only connection, so I did the only thing I knew to do. I shared the need via text and on my blog, and within hours, plans were lined up.

They would have somewhere to be on Christmas Eve, Christmas Day, and the days before and after. People swooped in, scooped them up, and showered them with gifts and experiences for their first Christmas in the United States.

Upon our return home, Fatima told story after story of their first Christmas, and how it had been a magical season filled with so much happiness.

"Alysa, there were toys for Abdul under trees, and a new shirt for me. We go to, how do you say, night before Christmas, like mosque?"

"Christmas Eve service at church?" I interjected.

"Yes, yes, Christmas Eve church with light you hold in hands. It was, how do you say, gentle?"

"Oh, a candlelight service. Was it peaceful?" I asked.

"Yes, that is the word. Peaceful. Too beautiful. I close eyes and breathe peace."

"Alysa, thank you too much for your friends. My best part is Abdul and I not alone. No forgotten and no scared. *Alhamdulillah*. Thanks be to God."

My friends brought light to the darkness surrounding Fatima and Abdul. Together is always better.

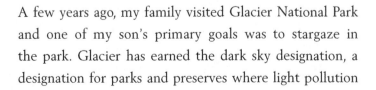

A few years ago, my family visited Glacier National Park and one of my son's primary goals was to stargaze in the park. Glacier has earned the dark sky designation, a designation for parks and preserves where light pollution is limited, giving unique opportunities to experience our universe.

We dropped Jack and Maddie off in the middle of nowhere, so they could hike into the back country for twenty-four hours, and then Jackson and I drove to the park at 10 p.m., and set up our sleeping bags and blankets. Jackson was on top of our borrowed 1985 green Suburban, and I was snuggled in a camping chair, waiting for the show.

That night at Glacier was exceptional. In the hours that followed, the sky began to show off, producing hundreds, then hundreds of thousands, and then millions of diamonds that cast light across the galaxy, almost too brilliant to behold.

We saw common constellations and, in time, the Milky Way revealed herself to us. As our eyes adjusted, shooting stars ripped across the sky in an old-fashioned game of tag. One of us would shout, "Did you see that one? Over to the left." And then within minutes another one would dart about like a rabbit being chased through a field. I lost track of the times we simultaneously yelled and pointed, "LOOK! OH MY GOODNESS! DID YOU SEE THAT?"

When we invited Fatima and Abdul into our family, and then into our circle of friends, it was a bit like that night sky.

We might have been the early stars on the horizon, but within weeks and months, Fatima and Abdul's darkness was illuminated by countless people who stepped forward to invite them into friendship.

Soon, their network expanded to a host of new friends that lit up their sky. One friend would arrange a playdate for Abdul, while another friend would drop by women's clothing, so Fatima would have appropriate attire for job interviews. A cluster of friends tasted her cooking and said, "You could start a catering business!" And then they proceeded to help her do just that.

We all shared our particular personalities, resources, and spheres of influence with Fatima, Abdul, and Layla, and in doing so, the Imperfect Welcome constellation produced joy and hope in each of us.

Welcome is contagious.

Maybe you enjoy these stories and feel your heart softening and a desire growing within. You might wonder where you could start.

I call it the Welcome Continuum, and as humans, we're all on it!

The Welcome Continuum

Rarely invite in **others**	Occassionally invite in **others**	Regularly invite in **friends**	Want to invite in **strangers**	Intentionally invite in **strangers**
1	2	3	4	5

The simplest place to start is all the way to the left on the continuum. Start by sharing one thing with one person. And if this is super scary, start by sharing something with someone you already know and love. Maybe you pick your grandmother up at the assisted living facility and bring her over for an afternoon of tea and cookies. Or maybe you share popsicles and the trampoline in your backyard each Wednesday afternoon for neighborhood friends and their kids. Start small.

Or maybe, you're a bit closer to the middle of the continuum and you feel as if you could invite a co-worker and her family over for dinner because they just moved to town from out-of-state and they really don't know anyone.

What could you share? What feels like a tiny step that you could manage?

Two questions guide our beginnings. Where will we start to show welcome to others this week/month? And where could that lead us in the months/years to come?

Here's the catch. Somewhere along our hospitality journey, as we move to the right on the Welcome Continuum, our sharing will shift from the tangible to the intangible. It will shift from learning to welcome (far left), to welcoming people we know and love (somewhere in the middle), to welcoming the acquaintance, the stranger, and the vulnerable (those on the right).

We start where we can and where we are. In time, and with practice, we move from sharing our stuff, to sharing ourselves. Vulnerability and the sharing of our stories builds the connection we all long for, and as we shuffle to the right on the continuum it may seem risky, but the reward is a beacon of hope, just like the brilliant night sky.

05

Did We Hide the Jewelry?

"There is no passion to be found playing small—in settling for a life that is less than the one you are capable of living. Take the risk."

Nelson Mandela

Alysa, I've never been to a white person's house. I'm nervous. Whatch y'all eat? What we fixin' to do when I'm there? Is your neighborhood safe?"

We had met Miss Betty months prior, during a season when Maddie was curious about homelessness. One sweltering hot July, while running errands, Maddie piped up from the back seat. "People that don't have houses probably like cupcakes, right, Mom?"

"Ya, I'm sure they do, Honey."

"Well then I want to make cupcakes and share them on my birthday. Can we do that?"

So that's what we did the day she turned seven. Maddie made the cupcakes that morning, pulling out all the seven-year-old stops, complete with store-bought icing, sprinkles, and food coloring.

When Jack finished work, we drove down to Breakthrough,[11] and met Miss Betty, Miss Terry, and many others. We asked them to celebrate Maddie's birthday with us, and the ladies were thrilled to do so. They loved Maddie's homemade cupcakes, grateful to have children in the building as it reminded them of their own at that age. Together we sang a rousing rendition of "Happy birthday dear Maddie, happy birthday to you!"

Have you ever met someone you just want to scoop up and take home because they're joy embodied? That was Miss Betty. She was vivacious, filled with a twinkly personality that led you to believe she was a handful, in the very best of ways. On subsequent visits to Breakthrough we would walk through the shelter doors, she would see Maddie and Jackson, and she would let out the most beautiful "Oooooooh, my babies!" and hobble over, welcoming their hugs and smiles. A grandma without much contact with her own grandbabies, she instantly fell in love with our kids, longing just to look at them as they sat beside each other at the shelter's tables. On many occasions, she tenderly reached out and touched their faces, as if transported to another season in her life.

We fell in love with her, and I think the love was mutual. We returned regularly, if for no other reason than to receive her hugs and hear her stories. She had a way of modeling for me the gift of slowing down and living present in each moment. She didn't take life for granted and remembered the good gifts the good Lord had given her through the decades.

Oh, how I wish you had met her. You would have enjoyed her love of simple pleasures: a drag of a cigarette in the courtyard while she watched Jackson and Maddie step up to the platform to play carpet ball; a sip of an ice-cold Coca-Cola in the shade on a hot summer afternoon; a bite of a warm chocolate-chip cookie dunked in coffee. She slowed down to enjoy life.

"Stop throwing the ball so hard, Maddie!" Jackson hollered.

"I'm not, Jackson," she retorted.

"Are too."

"Am not."

"Kids, you've only got each other, so you've gotta be kind. Now Maddie, go a little softer, and Jackson, mind your temper." Miss Betty would gently correct the kids as she stepped in, me at my wit's end, weary of their arguing yet again.

She was never in a rush—a balm for my hurried soul.

She regularly and without fanfare said, "Thank you, Jesus," when the kids would squeeze her tight. She was genuinely grateful that we stepped out of our whirlwind of activities to sit across the table from her. Sometimes we sat in silence and sometimes asked the latest on the status of her new housing paperwork, or if she had heard from her son that week. I'd ask about her children and she'd encourage me not to rush through the days when my kids were little. "I'd give anything to go back to those days and re-do some of them. I made a lot of mistakes, Alysa. Remember to say you're sorry; they'll forgive you."

A couple of months into our new friendship, we invited her over for an evening together in our home and she seemed very excited. Yet the day before, when I called to confirm, she would back out. This happened several times.

Eventually, she shared her real reason for canceling each time I'd call.

She was anxious.

"Alysa, where do y'all live? Do they see black people over by you? Is it gonna be okay, us drivin' home after dark?"

I walked her through what our time together might look like, complete with sitting around a table while eating roast beef and mashed potatoes. I'd have dessert—did she have a favorite? We simply wanted to visit, laugh, and swap stories. That's all.

I remember finishing our phone call and saying out loud to myself, "Didn't see that comin'! Wow, she's afraid to come to our house." In my ignorance, it never crossed my mind that *anyone* would be scared to come to *my* house or *my* neighborhood.

She finally came one chilly Saturday evening.

We picked her up at 4 p.m. on Carroll Avenue and we could tell she was nervous, so Jack pulled out his charm and humor and before long, she was laughing as we drove to our home in the Jefferson Park neighborhood of Chicago. The kids excitedly showed her around our main floor, Jackson taking her to see his Thomas the Train table in his room, and Maddie to see her latest crochet creation. We filled water glasses, ate, and asked lots of questions about what her life was like growing up on the west side of Chicago.

After dinner we sat on the couch in our front room, Maddie snuggled in tightly on one side while Jackson snuggled in on the other. As the evening progressed, Jackson spent time rolling trains all over the living room floor while we listened and told stories to each other. It's one of my favorite memories of Maddie. Her heart was bursting with excitement because Miss Betty had courageously walked through our front doors and into our home for supper. It was an evening of laughter and connecting, getting to know each other in the comfort of a home.

Maybe you, like me, have concerns around inviting others in. That's actually okay, and it's also very normal. There *are* things that feel scary to us when we start on this welcome journey. We may feel that our house isn't as nice as our friends', so why would we have people over—they'll just judge us. Perhaps letting people inside of our home feels too vulnerable, or it seems like too much work in a season when we're already running on empty. Or maybe we're introverted and we equate hospitality with noise and chaos.

If you had visited with my friend Melissa a few years back and asked about her thoughts on hospitality, she would have called herself a wimp. She had spent three years praying for a woman who struggled with homelessness and had encountered her in various settings. But fear and embarrassment over the size of her home kept her from offering more—of herself, her home, her family, and her finances. She didn't have a vision for how she could step in and connect, which kept her at a distance. She longed to help but fear made her timid.

One Thursday evening as a midwest snowstorm rolled in, Melissa and her family bumped into this same woman at their local Mexican restaurant. Melissa struck up her usual casual conversation and discovered that Anna—she finally discovered the woman had a name—wouldn't be able to make it to her shelter that night due to the impending storm.

Melissa shared,

> After about 30 seconds, I leaned in toward my husband and asked, "Can she stay in our basement?" He agreed immediately—he was going to ask me, but didn't want

to impose, as he knows the angst I have about our small house and having company. I'm not sure who was more shocked by the invite—Anna, my son, or myself!

We brought Anna home and when she entered, she broke down in tears. My house, full of unnecessary antiques, spoke "home" to her: "Oh, my mom and dad used to have a piano just like this," she cried as she tinkered out a tune. "Oh, this is just lovely! You are so lucky to live here!" she sputtered through tears.

Our home felt like her home—a refuge from the cold, isolation, and daily fight for survival. Our home was growing into its purpose, as my husband, son, and I were growing into ours. The following morning, when I took her a cup of coffee, she said she felt like a queen, sleeping in the most comfortable bed.

The seemingly common Friday morning hinted at the sacred, as I thought: The Lord slept in my basement last night, and was pleased, and this morning I'm serving him pancakes. It doesn't get much better than this.

God has a great sense of humor—or great timing. This all occurred after a week of feeling particularly sorry for myself and whining about "my small home." That night, after seeking prayer from a close group of friends, one friend pointed out: "Your home is a castle tonight."

Melissa had been entangled in the "What I have to offer is inadequate" excuse and almost missed out on God's invitation into kindness and friendship. Many of us struggle with similar limiting beliefs—that who we are and what we have to offer isn't enough.

Did you pick up on the gift it was for Melissa and her family to offer radical hospitality to a stranger? A warm, soft bed in exchange for a softened heart that was open to inviting others in. An issue—homelessness— became a person. Anna had her own personality, hopes, dreams, and fears. Anna and Melissa both became privy to the divine mystery of radical hospitality.

> *An issue— homelessness— became a person.*

One Sunday afternoon, while out with friends, I received several texts from Jack over a period of a few hours.

"I met a cool guy named Harry after church. He's living on the street and this dude needs a shower and his clothes washed. Is it okay if he comes over for the afternoon? I think I'll grill steak and let him crash for a few hours. Is that fine with you?"

"Sure. Sounds great. Have fun!"

Following were texts with photos of Harry on our couch with our dog, Coco, nestled in beside him. Coco can be high maintenance with newcomers, but Harry loves dogs, and he got down to her level and showed her some attention, so she immediately warmed to him.

After Harry showered and they got laundry started, Jack and Harry grilled steak, swapping stories as they ate until they were stuffed. Jack turned on the Big Ten Tournament, they settled in, and soon Harry fell fast asleep for hours with little Coco snuggled next to her new best friend. Jack snapped a photo of them curled up together and it's one of my favorites, because it captures welcome so perfectly. It's just a cozy brown blanket, a little dog, and an old man fast asleep on a basement sofa.

Later in the day, Jack texted and asked if it would be okay if Harry stayed the night, just to give him a break from life on the streets. Harry was a slow-moving, elderly grandfather, and Jack felt confident that, although he was a stranger, we would be safe.

Trusting Jack's assessment of our safety, and after meeting Harry later that day, I agreed that I was comfortable with him staying with us.

Did I sleep well that night? Not necessarily, but it was not because I was afraid. It was because I wanted to be wise. Our college-aged daughter was in Michigan, and our teenage son was now old enough to protect himself, but the mom in me still wanted to proceed with caution.

Did Jack move my jewelry? Yep. Not because we assumed Harry would steal, but just because that was a wise thing to do. As Jack likes to say, "I was born at night, but it wasn't last night."

The following morning, Harry came upstairs with gratitude for the gift of a soft bed, warm covers on a cold night, clean clothes to step into, and a sense of peace that allowed him to sleep soundly all night long. Our home became a space of respite for his weariness.

My cost? Just one night with less than stellar sleep.

Because it was a last-minute invitation, I was only able to offer him instant coffee (I know!), scrambled eggs, and toast. He received it as if I had spread a four-course meal before him. We sat together at the table, making small talk while he ate, and in the span of fifteen minutes he quietly offered up, "Thanks, Alysa. This is so good!" several times. He was genuinely grateful for this simple meal.

If we were to zoom out of that scenario, excuses, fear, and discernment were each present. I could have made the valid case for the fact that I was walking into a very busy week and didn't have time for the hours of extra work that would result in having to go to the laundromat to clean the heavy blankets Harry had used. The caution for my personal safety and the safety of my son were valid concerns, and had to be taken seriously. Harry was, after all, a complete stranger. Discernment is necessary. As we considered what we knew about Harry, we made the decision to proceed with caution, and invited him to stay the night.

We would be foolish not to weigh risks, yet at the same time, it can be easy to come up with a lengthy list of excuses as to why today isn't the day to extend an invitation. Maybe it's the fear of our stuff breaking, or of having an inadequate home, or having to drive to a sketchy part of town. Perhaps it is the worry of having nothing in common and not knowing what to say for three hours over dinner. Fear is natural and a necessary guard rail as we step into closer proximity with strangers.

Melissa and her family lost touch with Anna over the years, but like the Good Samaritan, they went where society said they probably shouldn't go. Melissa's fears were quieted through her proximity and connection with Anna over months of Thursday evening hellos at the local Mexican restaurant, which turned into weekly overnights at their home.

Stepping toward one another gave each of us a new picture of God.

When we welcomed Miss Betty, we welcomed "the other." Her age, race, socio-economic status, and her past and present, were radically different from ours. We had nothing in common. Each of us could have stayed apart if we had allowed our fears and excuses to dictate our actions, but stepping toward one another gave each of us a new picture of God.

I saw God through Betty's eyes in a way that I couldn't have seen him for myself if I had stayed on my side of town. Miss Betty believed that God was near to her, even in her affliction. I never heard her complain about her hardships; she owned her part in them, but also left allowance for the truth that sometimes hard things happen because we live in a broken-down world. Miss Betty called out to God with urgency. She *knew* she needed him every day, in every moment—she didn't just give lip-service to "needing" God. He was her lifeline. What an example to me, someone who struggles with self-reliance. She stood on God's promises and because of her, I have a more complete picture of who God is. It was in the proximity to diversity that I learned things I otherwise would not have learned about God. What a gift!

We wish our relationship with Miss Betty had continued over the course of many years, but she was only in our lives for a brief season. As is the transient nature often associated with homeless living, she moved on, and despite our best attempts we lost touch, leaving us saddened, but all the better for having known her.

I often think of Miss Betty. Her smile, her laughter, and the way she'd say my name. When I find myself driving on the West Side, I look out my window a bit more intently, as if I might stumble upon her again. I wonder where she's living, and I hope and pray that she is safe, warm, and in community.

Miss Betty, if, in some miraculous way, you read this, I want you to know I miss you and I love you. We all love you. So, so much.

06

Dirty Floors, Untidy Bathrooms, and Keeping Little People Alive

"Being heard is so close to being loved that for the average person, they are almost indistinguishable."

David Augsburger

need to tell you something. It's not good, and you probably won't want me in your family anymore."

Valerie (Val) said those words late one Friday night after the kids were in bed and the movie was over. She had lived with us off and on for years, and even after she had her own apartment in our neighborhood, she was over several times weekly for supper, to hang out, and just to be together.

I met Valerie in 1996 as her language arts and social studies teacher at Hillcrest School in Sentani, Irian Jaya, Indonesia. She was a shy 6th grader, but in time, her kind, tender, silly nature emerged. Six years later, after her high school graduation, she came to Chicago for college.

Jack and I married in 2000 and made our home in Chicago, so it was only natural that we would connect with her on weekends and holidays. For Valerie, being 9,800 miles from her family and childhood home in Indonesia, proved to be a difficult transition. Near the end of her college journey, she faced a dark cloud of depression and took a semester off, landing in our home for the month of January, 2006, while she figured out the next steps for her life. She flew to Indonesia in February and stayed through April, arriving back in Chicago in May, six weeks after our son Jackson was born.

The timing proved to be a mutual gift.

When our kids were little, I felt as if I were drowning, through no fault of theirs. Did you know that sleep deprivation is a tactic used against prisoners of war? That, and isolation. Early on, motherhood felt a bit like both to me. In exhaustion, at the end of each day, I felt anxious, thinking, *I can't do this for the next eighteen years*. I loved my sweet Maddie and Jackson with a fierce love, but good night! I was sleepy.

On top of regular motherhood, I was doing what women do—everything.

I co-led our local Mothers of Preschoolers (MOPS)[12] group, spoke occasionally at women's ministry meetings, and dropped off our almost four-year-old daughter to preschool each day by 7:45 a.m. Thank. You. Very. Much. I made meals, ran the house, tried to keep up with friends and family, chased my scrapbooking hobby, and generally tried to do it all. I screeched into meetings by the hair of my chinny-chin-chin, in our Chevy Malibu, Cheerio remnants and bright orange fishies all over the floorboard. I look back now and have compassion for my young mom phase. I was, indeed, a wreck, barely keeping it together. I had not yet learned the gift of slowing down, and while on the outside it appeared that I was thriving, my insides were shriveling like a raisin.

I brought it on myself because I couldn't say no, and I wanted to please all the people. Honestly, I liked the thrill of leading and accomplishing things, especially given the fact that mothering often felt like I was not accomplishing one thing. I would finish the dishes and throw in another load of laundry, only to turn around and see three cereal bowls, two sippy cups, and a partridge in a pear tree in the sink. Again.

When Valerie arrived back in Chicago later that spring, she asked if she could stay with us for a few months until school started back up that fall. After a rough spell in her own life, we had the space in our home and in our hearts.

She already seemed like our daughter, so we welcomed her home.

Auntie Val knew what she was getting when she walked up the steps and through our back door on any given day. She knew us and she knew our home, neither of which was perfect. I didn't realize what a gift that was to us.

She fit into our daily lives with no fanfare or confetti poppers. We weren't entertaining her, nor did she expect that. Val needed to belong to us, and we needed her to be okay with life how it was. In short order, we learned how we, too, needed to belong to her.

> An acceptance of imperfection is what makes hospitality sustainable and enjoyable.

On any random Wednesday, my imperfect hospitality looked like scrambled eggs for supper (once again) because I didn't execute the meal plan, because, well, follow-through on great ideas is my nemesis. Imperfect also looked like filthy kitchen floors and untidy bathrooms because I was keeping little people alive and didn't have time for such drivel. My imperfect meant my "office" was our dining room table with piles of paperwork strewn all over it for weeks on end.

Imperfect sums me up perfectly. And an acceptance of imperfection is what makes hospitality sustainable and enjoyable.

Valerie knew parts of our family life that no one else knew. She knew I lost my temper with the kids. Sadly, more regularly than I care to admit. She knew I served non-organic neon orange mac 'n cheese as a staple in their diet. She stepped over (and on) Thomas the Train tracks and cars. Every. Single. Day. She knew that as outgoing as I was, I was an introvert, which meant I couldn't Chatty Cathy it for endless hours at a time. I needed quiet. Peace and quiet, which could feel boring to some, but I had nothing extra to give in that season.

Because Valerie knew our imperfections, we felt free to welcome her in. We weren't playing a game to prove how great we were or how "together" we had it. She was right there in the 6th inning with us, hoping we would, by some miraculous act of God, still be standing at the end of the 9th.

She saw our imperfect, and it didn't scare her.

Somehow, she still loved us.

To this day, she looks back with great love on her years with us. "I knew you messed up, and that actually made me feel better about myself. It felt safe. I belonged and you all loved me as if I were your very own. That was never in question."

Imperfection offered freedom to all of us.

Making room for being imperfect around others is the key to sustaining a life of hospitality. If we long for a spirit of welcome to define who we are, then we have to say goodbye to perfection, like the way we long to say goodbye to those extra pounds on January 1st each year.

Imperfection enables sustainability over the decades.

As life would have it, our Maddie was an early bird, as in 5:30 a.m. early. Every day of the live-long week. Because having Auntie Valerie in the house was exciting, Maddie would often run up to her room to see if they could go butterfly hunting, or out on a walk around the neighborhood, or read a book together on the couch. Valerie graciously tended to my need for sleep (remember, I had an infant), by helping with Maddie most mornings. This set-up worked because Val had become part of our family years prior, and in her love for us, she pitched in.

In those early days of mothering, I silently and semi-regularly complained to myself that I didn't have my mom nearby like so many of my friends. It wasn't fair. They could drop off their child at Grandma's when they had to go to a dentist appointment, or they could swing by for supper when they didn't have a meal ready at their own home. I was pretty good at feeling sorry for myself and remember thinking: *I wish I had regular help. Like everyday help. Must be nice.*

And then one afternoon, I was sitting on our couch feeding Jackson for what felt like the 17th time that day, when I glanced out the window and saw Maddie and Val creating masterpiece art with chalk on our front sidewalk. I realized in that moment that God had sent me help.

Her name was Auntie Val.

As the prophet Isaiah says about God, "He tends his flock like a shepherd: He gathers the lambs in his arms and carries them close to his heart; he gently leads those that have young."[13]

We were a good pair, Valerie and I.

While Jack worked outside the home, I worked at keeping two little people alive on the regular, as Valerie tried to make sense of childhood trauma that clung to her soul like sand on a wet towel at the beach. For years her heart was heavy as she mourned pieces of her past as they mingled with pieces of her present. Our talks about God and doubt, faith and missions, wounds we had suffered, some even by family or friends, and everything in-between, are some of the most honest conversations I've ever had. Nothing was off the table with Val.

We listened to each other.

She listened as I regularly shared my fears of messing up my kids through daily failures marked by repeated impatience. I felt that I wasn't a good enough mom—whatever that even means—and I was fraught with overwhelming expressions of insecurity in my role as a mother.

And I listened to her as she healed and figured out who she was apart from her family of origin and all she had ever known—life as a third-culture kid.[14]

Neither of us had all the answers, but we could listen.

Can I let you in on a little secret? While my listening was, I'm sure, helpful to a degree, guess who helped her heal the most? Maddie and Jackson. They were each a soothing balm to her aching heart. They loved her unconditionally and with profound delight. They ran to her when she walked in the door the way our little dog Coco scampered to us every time we returned home. They fought over who she should hug first, and she always had to sit in the middle of the couch because they *each* had to be beside her. They proudly made artwork that she displayed as if Picasso him-self had hand-delivered the piece. She was the aunt who lived with us, which forged a strong bond that lasts to this day.

There is nothing quite so grounding as knowing you belong.

She belonged to them, and they to her. There is nothing quite so grounding as knowing you belong.

In time, Valerie flew the coop to get married and move to Virginia. We arrived days before the grand festivities, helping with set up and such, and I had the honor of photographing her wedding. (Side-note: It is hard to take photos when you're crying.)

The tears were ones of pride as Valerie had blossomed over the years, before our very eyes. She had grown from that young, insecure, depressed and fearful teenager, to the struggling-with-who-she-was young adult, into the beauti-ful bride who walked into the tiny country church that warm October afternoon.

She had changed.

The small wooden benches on either side of the center aisle held those who loved Valerie most, and she was pre-ceded down the aisle by both of our children, her atten-dants for the day. I would argue that never was there a family, that wasn't technically a family, closer to the beautiful bride.

Incidentally, the opening bit of this chapter, the part where she said, "I need to tell you something. It's not good and you probably won't want me in your family anymore," was a shame-based story she was telling herself. Belonging, one of our greatest hopes, can become one of our biggest fears when we make mistakes—which we all do. Shame has this sneaky way of worming its way into the stories we tell ourselves, and the story she told herself that night was, "If I mess up, I will lose their love. And I messed up, so I guess this is it. They're not going to want me any longer."

As tears fell from her eyes in confession that night, I remember thinking, *Sweet daughter, nothing could ever make us stop loving you. None of us is perfect and you, of all people, should know how imperfect we are. You belong to us. And we belong to you. Always and forever.*

07

I See You

"The world doesn't need another copy of someone else; the world needs you."

Bob Goff

t was a large auditorium. Thousands of participants were at the conference, and yet I felt as if I were the only one in the room. Have you ever experienced that? The speaker's words pierced: "What is *your* problem to solve? What keeps *you* up at night? What grabs *your* attention when it comes across your news feed? What is that holy fight in you that bubbles up where you just *have to* step in and help?"[15]

You and I are different, right? We have different

personalities, quirks, values, passions, and priorities. We live in different homes, cities, and cultures. We have different occupations, families of origin, and experiences.

And because of that, what captures my heart might not capture yours. We are different because of God's perfect, creative design, and we all have something to offer.

Who captures your heart?

At every turn I saw kids: orphans in need of adoption, children who needed tutoring in our local public school, those who needed foster care. I saw the billboards and television ads, and my heart ached because of all the hurts in the world. Harm and hurt inflicted on children feels unbearable to me.

And then I became a mom.

And in the exhaustion that holds hands with mothering those first few years, I could not take care of other people's kids. During that season, I rarely swapped babysitting with friends because that would involve being responsible for keeping more little people alive. I didn't want to volunteer in the church nursery because, well, I was CEO, manager, and night shift worker of my own personal daycare.

For years I was bound by guilt over the seemingly self-ish nature of only wanting to take care of my own kids. My love was—and is—fierce for them, but I had nothing left to give kids in need.

I lost sleep over this.

In tandem with this internal tension, our daughter begged us to host a Safe Families child. Here's the thing:

I desperately wanted to host a child because I knew the need and I felt deep compassion, but the thought of bringing someone else's child into our home overwhelmed me. So much so, that over the years I repeatedly said no to our daughter's request.

Have you felt that way before? You see a need, you know you could meet the need, and then you choose not to meet the need. Then guilt creeps in like a burglar at midnight.

The chatter inside my head was deafening. *You're a stay-at-home mom, Alysa. What's one more kid? You have extra rooms in your home. You have money enough to feed extra mouths. You have bins of off-season and off-sized clothes in your attic. Toys? Good night! You have toys for all ages and stages, and you could start a library with all the children's books you own. What is your problem? Kids are literally dying around the globe and you can't even open up your home to one more kid? Golly, you're selfish.*

I cannot fully express how long I wrestled with this tension.

In time, something inside me shifted and I decided to try. By spring of 2014, I had stepped out of survival mode as my own kids were getting older, which made day-to-day parenting easier. *I can do anything for a couple of months, right?* I was finally ready.

Omari, an almost two-year-old boy, arrived in August 2014. He was a stranger to us, and we learned that his mom needed someone to care for him so she could focus on getting the help she needed.

Maddie was twelve and was thrilled that we were going to host a child. She pulled out a blanket she had made specifically for her first Safe Families child and prepared the house to receive the little boy. She had different stations set up around our home: a book station, one for crafts, a separate area for toys, a place for his clothing, and a changing area complete with diapers and wipes. Her excitement was uncontainable.

Our eight-year-old son, on the other hand, responded to the news with, "Oh boy. Young ones take SOOOO much attention. And I am NOT changing any diapers." (*emphasis his*)

A few nights later, in the quiet of the bathroom, while brushing his teeth, Jackson whispered to me, "Mom, I love Omari."

Omari was a popsicle on a hot summer day, even though he bit like an alligator and scratched like a tiger. He dropped the F-bomb daily, and b*tch was one of his favorite words; you would have thought he was a 19-year-old wartime sailor on the USS Missouri. Seriously, friends, he was hard core.

Yet, we quickly fell in love with him.

Omari spent six weeks with us that summer. We passed the days with long walks to the neighborhood park and hours on the couch as Maddie and I read countless books to him. We took pictures and texted his mother regularly so that she knew he was in a safe and loving environment. He missed her but he was also thriving.

He went on vacation with us and experienced his first of many boat rides, and squealed as Papa sped across the waters of Gull Lake, Michigan. He went on turtle hunts and scooped up buckets of sand to plop on the dock, and he ran through the sprinkler as Jackson chased after him. He was a kid being a kid.

But caring for someone else's kid can be hard. Jack tells this story:

> Everyone was out, so I was on Omari duty. At first it was fine, but I could see Omari was tired, and getting restless and cranky. I tried to get him interested in a toy but he wasn't having it. His bottle—nope. He grew increasingly cranky. His diaper was clean so I tried distracting him with something else. "F*ck," he shouted, as he scratched me.
>
> Snap went my fragile emotional psyche.
>
> What recourse do you have when it's not your child? Unsure what to do, I got up and started the mountain of dishes that were waiting in the kitchen. Omari continued to curse and wail.
>
> Soon after, the back door opened, and Maddie walked in to what I'm sure was an electric scene, with Omari laying on the floor, screeching and swearing, and me standing over a pile of dirty dishes with a panicked "save me" look in my eyes.
>
> She immediately recognized what was happening and sprang into action. She picked up Omari just as he

was wearing himself out. She played peek-a-boo and within a couple minutes, got him laughing. In an hour it was bedtime, and before I knew it, she had tucked him into his crib.

Maddie was reading in her room later that night when I walked in, reached into my back pocket, pulled out my wallet, and grabbed a twenty. I placed it on her night stand, slid it over to her, turned, and walked out of the room without saying a word.

Perhaps not my best parenting moment, but sometimes, we all just need some help.

When we initially stepped into the host family role I told myself I would commit to one placement. I would see how it went and if I could do it again. *Or not.*

This commitment was scarier to me than all the other opportunities we had taken to help strangers. I am intrigued by the fact that this was so daunting to me. You might be curious as well because perhaps you're thinking that you could totally help kids and that would be no big deal. You already have three kids so why not add a fourth. But to help a refugee from another country? No way!

While our time caring for Omari was much easier than I anticipated, and there were plenty of moments of great joy, it was still challenging for me. At the end of his placement, I knew this wasn't going to be something I could continue to do, but I needed to confirm that truth by at least trying.

For Maddie's sake, in an effort to nurture her

compassionate heart, I had wanted to provide that opportunity for her, and for us as a family. I also needed to be open to the possibility that God could surprise me and give me the ability to step in and parent another child. What if God had something amazing in store for me and I missed it because I wasn't even willing to try?

> *What if God had something amazing in store for me and I missed it because I wasn't even willing to try?*

At the end of the experience I decided I couldn't do it again. Or at least, during that season. And that's okay, right? It didn't mean I couldn't help Safe Families in other ways because it is an amazing organization doing amazing things around the globe. We're called to help others, and we need to do something, but we can't do everything.

Welcome looks different for all of us.

Ruth and Ken are welcomers. They are MorMor (Norwegian for mother's mother) and Boppy (a family name for grandpa) to dozens of kids who aren't their grandkids, my own included. They live a life of welcome.

Maybe you know the type. The lady with the kind eyes and easy smile who sits beside you while you're waiting for a table at the restaurant. Before long, she notices your darling children and comments on how well-behaved they are, leading to a general discussion about motherhood and the ups and downs of various stages. Maybe it's the gentleman in the sporting store who sees you looking at golf clubs, and he jokes about his own need for new clubs to improve his game.

We each get to bring our distinctive selves to the world of hospitality.

We're all uniquely wired and God needs each of us to do our part—the Hallers doing their part, the Clarks doing theirs, and you doing yours. We each get to bring our distinctive selves to the world of hospitality.

Ruth and Ken are curious by nature and adventurous at heart. That is how they are uniquely wired. Years ago, they decided to carry a simple business card with their personal information on it, to give away when they meet new friends. (It goes without saying that they use discretion in distributing their card.)

They live ten minutes from O'Hare—one of the world's busiest airports—so whether cruising in the Caribbean, dining in South America, or strolling through a European city, they pass cards out to trusted taxi drivers, wait staff, and new friends alike, an open invitation to call if others find themselves wandering through Chicago.

One evening as Ken and Ruth were driving home from Minnesota, they received a call from a young man.

"Do you remember me? My name is James, and you gave

me your card a few months ago. I'm on the Greyhound bus headed to Chicago. Could I stay with you tonight?"

"Sure! We're not home, but will be in a few hours. Here's our address: grab a cab, and we'll meet you there."

After hanging up, Ken and Ruth looked at each other, chuckled, and realized they had no idea who this guy was, but tonight they'd be meeting him again and hosting him in their home. Ruth's take on new friendship? "It's an adventure to get to know somebody and how they live. You learn from other people. It's just fun."

Their guest arrived, and as he stepped out of the cab, walked up their sidewalk, and removed his hat, it dawned on Ruth. "Oh, I remember him now! He was our waiter when we were on Mackinac Island last summer."

Curious to hear more about his life in Africa, they ordered pizza for supper, sat around their kitchen table, and asked him all sorts of questions. He was a participant in a work exchange program in which college-aged students from other countries come to the United States to work for a year.

Before long they found themselves on the couch with their South African friend between them, his laptop open, showing photo after photo of his world back home. They took the time to ask questions and look at the photos, learning about his family, home town, traditions, and culture.

This all started with intentionality: one couple created a business card with personal information so they could offer welcome, should the need ever arise.

After only twenty-four hours together, as James left the next day, headed home to South Africa, his simple words touched Ruth and Ken. "I don't know what I would have done without you."

Their invitation, coupled with curiosity, led to mutual friendship and they still connect with James and his family today—several years later—over email. I continue to be amazed by the profound impact and lasting gift an invitation makes.

Ruth shared that some might think, "I'd never bring someone to my home from South Africa that I only met for ten minutes months ago." But for them, it is worth it.

This story epitomizes the Imperfect Welcome. Ruth and Ken didn't initially remember the guy, but they knew that, if they had given him a business card, they had previously connected with him. They had been gone for a long weekend and were just rolling back into town themselves. Weary from a seven-hour drive, they had few groceries in the house, and it would have been understandable for them to simply say that they couldn't host the man later that night. They could wish him well and hope that he had a safe trip back to Africa.

And yet, they *could* say yes. They could order take-out, quickly change the guest-room sheets, and offer a shower and a warm bed. They could offer their time, themselves, and a safe place for this stranger to land.

And they did.

"I don't know what I would have done without you."

Let that sink in.

Some years later, they received an email with a photo of James, his wife, and their infant son. The subject line on the email? "You're grandparents!"

All because Ken and Ruth decided to make it their practice to welcome others into their lives. All because they said yes to a man passing through Chicago.

Ruth and Ken gather people as you and I might gather seashells on our first trip to the ocean. They love people and they love to study other cultures, and find that welcoming people is one of the greatest joys they experience—which is exactly how God wired them. They welcome because that's who they are.

Meet my dear friend, Kristin. To date, her family has hosted over forty children through Safe Families in their home, from a weekend stay to a three-year placement. Whether picking up a newborn at the hospital or opening up their home to siblings for a few weeks, theirs is a revolving door.

Much the same way we felt called to come alongside refugees, Kristen, Ken, and their daughters knew that they wanted to open their home—and themselves—to children who needed temporary care.

I sat across from Kristin last year, peppering her with questions.

"Why help kids and their parents?" I asked.

"Well, back in 2009, we sat in a church meeting and heard about the need for loving families to sign up, and by the end of that meeting we knew we wanted to host children as a way to help their parents. We have a place at our table and empty rooms in our home, and we wanted to keep families together. We figured if we could step into a crisis to help take care of the kids, that might keep the family intact in the long run."

"Wow. I love that concept of having room at your table and in your home, which translates to having room in your hearts," I said. "I know there's a cost to serving, and I have felt that cost myself. But at some point, the kids leave your home and that has to be painful to become attached and then let them go. Why do you do that to yourselves, knowing there's pain at the end of most placements?"

Her answer? "It isn't always easy, but I don't think ease is the goal of serving, right? Our family goes into each new placement knowing our hearts might be broken, but we attach to the child because that's what the child needs. We're called to love kids for the time we have them and we can do that. We have love to give."

We have love to give.

As if that wasn't enough, she went on to say, "We found in the times that hurt the most, the best way to heal was simply to bring in another child. To open up again. We attach. We love. We nurture. We let go. We repeat."

Mic drop.

As for me, I learned a few years ago that I can offer hospitality in a lot of ways, but what I'm passionate about and what I'm really good at, is coming alongside those who need a place to belong. That's where joy and excitement collide inside of me, an experience that fills rather than depletes.

I look back fondly on our time with Omari, and know that it was a necessary step in my personal journey. He was a gift to us and he brought loads of laughter to our home. And every so often, years later, we wonder how he is and what he is up to. Today he would be almost twelve. That's hard to believe.

Want to know what kids think about all of this?

Greta, twenty-three, shared this: "My family decided to open our home and take in kids who needed help, and that has been life-changing for me. Kids that stayed with us felt like our family, whether they were with us for a few nights or two years. When I'm older, I am committed to opening my home to kids that need help because I know the immense effect it had on me. I want my kids to grow up in an environment like I did, with strangers sleeping in the next room because I think that's how I encountered Jesus as a kid."

And Klara, twenty-one, shared this: "Seeing my parents open up our home to others has shown me what it is like to care for God's children who might not get the same love and attention anywhere else. I will forever be grateful for the different ages and cultures we have let into our hearts and our home. I have learned so much from them. My parents' selfless and loving hearts taught me to be the person I am today."

Want to know a little something?

Greta and Klara's parents are Kristin and Ken. And Kristin's parents are Ruth and Ken, MorMor and Boppy.

Does living a life of welcome impact our kids? Our grandkids? Oh, sweet friends, I hope you see the direct connection. How we live our lives has a profound impact on the lives of the following generations. The Imperfect Welcome models for our children—and fosters in us—a spirit of other-centeredness. When we focus on others, we assign worth to them, attending to that piece in each of us which is made in God's image and longs for connection—with each other and with God. And isn't that what this is all about?

> Hospitality says, "I see you."

Hospitality says, "I see you."

So, with the love that we each have to give, who could we "see" today?

Note: See 'Appendix B: What Kids Are Saying' for more stories from kids whose parents made welcome a way of life.

08

Dancing in a Safe House

"After nourishment, shelter and companionship, stories are the thing we need most in the world."

Philip Pullman

We heard and smelled the campfires and roasting pits long before we caught a glimpse of the thousands of people milling around picnic tables, blankets, and the forest preserve pavilion.

Our Iranian friend Tahmina invited us to a Persian New Year party on a cloudy March afternoon. We thought it was to be a small family picnic in the forest preserve with her, her three young girls, and a couple of her friends.

We stepped out of our car as a dozen others jockeyed

for places to park within a quarter mile of the party. Old and young balanced chairs, coolers, and babes in arms, and searched for their families amidst the crowd.

As we walked closer, people reconnected and greeted others with side-to-side kisses and squishy hugs. It was as if butterflies flitted about in a beautiful wildflower field, not sure where to land. The motion, electric hum, and cultural vibe in St. Paul's Woods were intoxicating, and as we approached, we shook our heads and chuckled at the adventure we had stumbled into.

We had no idea.

Middle Eastern music crackled from the DJ's speakers set atop a gray plastic folding table under the pavilion. Jangling with excitement, folks danced with arms circling, and fingers playing mini cymbals. Scarves on swaying hips moved with ease as friends shouted in Farsi over breaks in the music, heads thrown back in laughter. I had only seen gatherings like this in movies.

When we found Tahmina, she pulled us into the experience, and we danced to the best of our Western abilities. As we busted our moves, the crowd busted their guts. We were something to behold.

We knew exactly four people at the start of the celebration, but in mere minutes we were swallowed up into the scene, as if we were long-lost relatives coming home after decades away.

In need of a break, we squeezed through the crowd, and as we made our way to the side, we saw an older gentleman wave us over. He motioned in the air with a plastic spoon, excited to point to the large bowl of steaming hot liquid in front of him.

"Would you like to try?" he nodded to the bowl with his chin.

I turned to Jack with eyebrows raised and then, with a courteous smile, I looked back at the man. "Sure, thank you so much. It smells wonderful."

Internally, we had questions. *Who is this guy? What is this? How do we get out of finishing this if it's gross?* Back in Indonesia at a holiday party, wanting to be culturally sensitive, I ate dog meat, so this invitation felt like dangerous territory.

We lucked out! It was delicious!

It didn't feel right to arrive empty-handed. It was a potluck, but they assured us, "It's okay. Eat, eat. We'll share."

People moved methodically amidst the chaos. The saffron rice bowl was scooched next to the yogurt and diced cucumbers, while someone else rummaged through a grocery store bag to find utensils. The hummus made its way to the naan (Persian bread); meanwhile, grandmothers shouted instructions to the younger generation who stoked the coals and skewered the beef and lamb to ready the shish kabobs.

They invited us, strangers, to their table with grand sweeps of "help yourself." And though we had nothing to offer but a smile and a curiosity about their traditions, that was apparently enough. We took it in, grateful for our connection to Tahmina and by extension, this cultural experience. We were welcomed as if we were one of them.

Over the past eight years, new-to-me parts of Tahmina's story continue to surface. If you knew even a portion of it, you would be impacted every time you were with her because, humanly speaking, there is no reason she's a) still standing, and b) standing with joy. It doesn't make sense, except that it makes perfect sense because of God's miraculous rescue in her life.

Tahmina is one of the most inspiring women I have ever known. Her story of courage, and her ability to persevere—with joy—in the face of horrific trials has no rivals. When I'm tempted to feel sorry for myself, I think of Tahmina. When I want to give up, I see her strength, and it inspires me to push forward.

In 2011, courage to leave her home culture welled up deep within. In search of escape from a wildly abusive husband, where Tahmina felt caged, yet unseen, she made her plan. She knew her male-dominated culture wouldn't provide protection, so she gathered up her three young children, packed a simple bag, tucked the beauty of her culture and the memories of a lifetime into her heart, and murmured forever goodbyes to all she had ever known—her land, her home, and her family. She knew she would never return, and the ache was nearly unbearable as the weight of her forever goodbye set a new dance in motion.

By cover of night and fearful for their lives, she journeyed up and over the last pass of the Zagros mountain range with her children and younger brother, who had volunteered to accompany them on their escape. Soldiers lurked in the darkness as she stumbled precariously close to cliff edges while balancing a child in her arms. Terror nipped at her heels, motivating every step, one foot in front of the other, hour after hour. Desperation was driving her actions, as she could no longer stay in bondage.

After traveling all night, the Turkish border was within reach. The invisible line was her ticket to freedom—the longed-for escape from a life of horrific abuse. She, her children, and her brother made their final run for the border, and as they crossed to freedom, they collapsed into the arms of strangers who stood ready to welcome arriving refugees.

She struggled those first few weeks. She didn't know the language, struggled to find consistent work, and saved every bit she could. She managed to bring some money with her from Iran, but would need more to reach their final destination.

Through hard work and determination, she found a handler who agreed to assist her in safe passage to Europe. She studied his eyes and tried to determine if he was trustworthy. Unsure but without other options, she nervously handed over virtually all the money she had worked so hard to earn and save.

That was the last she saw of him. He disappeared with their money and their hope.

Now what?

In one of the lowest points in her life, alone and afraid, Tahmina stumbled into a Catholic church and happened to meet Sister Anna. In gentleness, this woman shared the love of God with her and showed her God's promise to never leave Tahmina, if she would choose to trust him. God whispered hope to Tahmina through the loving-kindness of Sister Anna.

"Alysa, I met Jesus Christ exactly when my money was stolen. Sister Anna was an angel to me and the kids. From then on, my heart was full of love, and I no longer had to worry. I knew God would protect me. And he has, even now."

"Sister took me to the police, and when I told them about my husband and the abuse, and then the robbery, they said they could help. While they could not find my stolen money, they could bring us to safety, where I could learn the language and they would pay for our food and shelter."

"Whatever you did for one of the least of these brothers and sisters of mine, you did for me,"[16] says Jesus. Apparently, Sister Anna took him at his word.

Because of her vulnerability and the threat of her husband (he was still actively searching for her), Tahmina was whisked away to a secret location and confined with strangers in an even stranger land. She crouched within a walled complex, not sure where she was or how long she would be there. When would this nightmare end?

It turns out that she was in a safe house, shoulder-to-shoulder with other women of varied cultures, who had also run for their lives. Most—if not all—were beaten and threatened by husbands, which led them to this room with no view. While they were safe from immediate danger by the men in their lives, they were left desperate for hope and new beginnings.

The air was rife with cigarette smoke, body odor, fear, and hopelessness. The trauma each had endured spilled out onto the other women in the shelter. They fought over which station to watch on their 13-inch community television, and faces were scratched and voices screeched as women pushed and shoved to find space in the room. It was every woman for herself.

"Alysa, my kids sat at my feet, and I could hardly believe that I had taken them from all they had ever known to this. We were confined to a room with mad women. All I wanted was for my children to have a normal, safe life," she shared.

In the weariness of this new normal, Tahmina hit her breaking point.

One night after supper, in an act of courage and in an effort to connect with the other women, she stood up in front of all the other ladies.

She started talking. "I was beaten and abused by my husband for too many years. Maybe this sounds familiar to you? Just a few weeks ago, I knew I had to be brave for my children, so we sneaked away forever."

Quiet settled into the room, and ears tuned into her pain as she shared her journey to freedom. Whispers of empathy gently bounced off the walls as tears slid down cheeks. There was a mutual language spoken that night in that room filled with hurting women. It was the language of understanding. Compassion settled in hearts that were once fraught with crass language and crazed behavior.

There, in the middle of telling her story, healing marched in.

There, in the middle of telling her story, healing marched in.

Proximity plus authenticity promotes transformation. In all of us. "Story" connects us to other places and cultures, and a good story can produce hope on dark days when we feel prone to giving up or giving in to whatever it is that has a hold on us.

There is a tender understanding—a "me too" transaction—that is exchanged when we lean in close and listen to the stories our hearts long to tell. It is in the telling of our stories that we are nudged toward healing and hope.

The next evening, as she switched the television set to

off, Tahmina pulled a random woman up in front. "Okay. Your turn. Tell your story."

And so it went on for days. Weeks, even. And in the sharing and the listening, the climate within the walls of the safe house drastically changed.

And then?

The dancing started.

Tahmina, a celebrator extraordinaire, decided one night that it was time to dance. As only Tahmina can do, she led with joy and encouraged women to join. Laughter filled the room as women doubled over in fits of giggles, attempting new and old dance moves alike, with hands joined and hearts mending. Spinning and twirling, there in the simplest of rooms, nations were brought together as courage promoted more courage.

She eventually arrived in Chicago in September of 2013, where we met through a family from our church who, like us a few years prior, had decided to volunteer with World Relief.

I have so many memories with Tahmina, and they all include her infectious joy. Some are big parties, and some include regular life together. She has a silly streak about her, so on more than one occasion we've giggled as one of us has tripped over a crack in the sidewalk or dribbled sauce on our shirt as we ate. We both laugh easily and often, so our friendship feels natural. Whether we are working through housing forms and parking tickets, or trying to relocate her family to Canada under refugee status, or waiting for the community college admissions office to pick up the phone, we always find a reason to laugh.

One Monday afternoon a few months ago, Tahmina texted:

"Alysa, let's go out for tea this week. I've found the perfect place that has wonderful teas like back home, and I would like to treat you."

Shortly after ten o'clock in the morning, Tahmina, tall and slender, strolled along the sidewalk in her fancy sunglasses, long coat, and knee-high boots, with an air of confidence that matched her lengthy stride.

I stepped out of my car, and in true Tahmina fashion, she squealed with delight and rushed to hug me while we kissed cheeks from side to side. If you've met her, you have felt her strong embrace, smelled her sweet perfume, and been the recipient of her love because that is who she is.

Tahmina loves people.

We stepped inside the shop to find that it was restricted to take-out only due to an on-site construction project. Hmmm. Not what we anticipated, as our goal was a leisurely visit at a café table over a hot cup of specialty tea. But, as we both do, we settled on plan B.

There we were, sitting in my teeny, two-door 2006 Hyundai Accent, affectionately named Austin, feeling as if we had been stuffed into a shoebox on wheels.

She jumped right in and asked how Maddie was doing at college, which led to talking about her kids. And back and forth we went, like a 1980s teeter-totter, as we caught up on the latest random questions we had for each other since our last visit a couple of before.

"Tahmina, tell me more about the first few weeks you arrived in Chicago. I don't remember some of the particulars. How did you manage, with three little girls, not really knowing the language back then, not having a job, and being all alone?" I asked.

Tahmina shared,

> When I arrived, I bumped into a gorgeous Iranian woman at the grocery store, and she invited me to a party on Devon Avenue. So close to my house. I didn't know her, but because she spoke my language and knew my culture, I was desperate to visit with her. When I arrived at the party that evening, I quickly knew this was not a good situation. We said hello and she pulled me aside, and when no one was watching, she opened the pocket in her coat. She offered me heroin.
>
> "No. I don't do that! NO!" I told her.
>
> The lady leaned in tight and whispered, "But if you sell it, you can get rich. It will help you take care of your kids here in America. You don't have to use it yourself, just sell it. It will be good for you to do that. It's easy."
>
> She tried to convince me, but I refused.

I sat stunned. This was the first time I was hearing this piece of her story, and it reminded me, yet again, of the vulnerability we all face when we are in new, unfamiliar settings. Her story could have easily gone sideways from day one, yet she had courage to do the right thing in the face of adversity.

"Tahmina, that's so scary. What did you do?"

"I found my kids (they were in a different room with other children), and told them we had to go. They fussed and wanted to stay but I said, 'We must go now!' We walked out of her home and I never looked back."

"Wow. I can't even, Tahmina. You are so strong and courageous to start over in a new land and a new culture. All alone. And then to face that immediately after you arrived!"

"Alysa, that's when I realized that I am a little fish in a big ocean, and there are a million dangerous sharks. You have no idea! I was lost. God came at the right moment in my life. When I was hiking over the mountains, running for my life, I was scared. Crossing the border to Turkey, I was scared. But when I came to Chicago, I was terrified!"

"I remembered what Sister Anna taught me, and I remembered the miracles I saw with my own eyes. You know, the Middle East is very small and different from the United States, but Jesus never left us alone. He is still with us, even now."

There we sat in my car, in a suburb of Chicago, far removed from the Middle East. We were just two friends visiting over tea, sharing memories of life's ups and downs.

A few years back I was asked, "Who has made a significant impact on your faith journey in recent years?"

The first person who came to my mind?

Tahmina.

I met her during a particular season when I was low on joy and high on discontentment. I was weary, in need of encouragement, and a general swift kick in the pants. Ever been there?

Without even know-ing it, simply being around her motivated me to move through circumstances with joy, hope, and courage, instead of despair, discontentment, and discouragement.

In the sharing of her story, I found hope in the middle of mine.

It's remarkable, really.

In the sharing of her story, I found hope in the middle of mine.

The Imperfect Welcome feels like how I imagine the Garden of Eden felt as God visited with Adam and Eve. A bit of the Kingdom of Heaven coming down to Earth.

In God's perfect design, there is room for our imper-fect belonging to each other. An invitation leads us to where connection and belonging co-mingle as a foretaste of heaven. Yes, we can help a new friend who needs rela-tionship, or we can share our network of friends, or maybe we can offer something tangible, like a place to stay when someone passes through town. But the gift is mutual: friendship, encouragement, connection, transformation, and great joy. Who knows, maybe next year you'll end up dancing to Persian music at an Iranian New Year's party.

09

United Nations Easter

*"There is a common sense that something holy,
something transformational,
something grace-filled happens at the table."*

Larry Goodpaster

Unless I'm in a really rough head space, I can usually reframe anything and everything. It's my superpower.

The bus breaks down in Germany. *We're in Germany on vacation, so who cares? And at least we made it to a rest area instead of breaking down on the side of the autobahn.* The waiter showed up with fried chicken instead of grilled chicken on the salad. *Fantastic. Fried always tastes better anyway!* I didn't know any of the songs we sang in church this morning. *But now we know four new ones that have cool grooves and amazing lyrics.* This traffic is brutal. *But we have Sting and a smokin' stereo system. And the air is warm and the sunroof is open.*

So, what if we reframed the concept around hospitality from a "must do" to a "get to do?" A mindset shift: instead of work to do, there is a story to enter. Instead of an infringement on "me time," what if connection is gained through "we time?"

We all get to practice hospitality according to the unique way God designed us. No matter who we are, we can welcome. Let's work within the framework of our strengths to care for others and their burdens. The Imperfect Welcome isn't meant to be an obligatory response to a need we see. It's not about checking the 'I served someone today' box off our to-do lists. It's about joy in the coming together as we welcome others into our everyday rhythms.

In January of 2022, I signed up to be a transportation volunteer through World Relief. The coordinator would email a list of immigrant and refugee needs for the following week, and volunteers simply clicked on the appointments they could fulfill. I knew I could offer a few hours each week to be friendly while I helped meet a small need. Whether it was to bring refugees to doctor's visits or the like, it was an easy way to step toward others in their time of need, and it worked within the confines of my schedule.

Idania, an immigrant from Honduras, alone and seven

months pregnant, left everything she knew and traveled mostly on foot over rocks, trails, and rivers to come to the United States. Life was so dangerous in her home country that she felt it worth the risk to make the long trek north. She eventually arrived in Chicago and within a short while gave birth to Rosa, a baby girl.

I met Idania that January and enjoyed driving her to various appointments over the winter months. We struck up a friendship and before long we invited her to our home. She was lonely, hungry for friendship.

I called her one afternoon in March. "Hey Idania, we're having some people over for Easter in a few weeks and we would love to invite you, Rosa, and your Honduran friends. Could you join us?"

She excitedly offered to bring Honduran food, and I added, "That sounds amazing! We'll pick you up and you can plan to spend the day with us! Bring comfy shoes because we always go for a walk after lunch, before dessert!"

"¡Que divertido! How fun!" she replied.

Easter is when I reframe the most.

Realistically, it's a lot of work to host 20-30 people in our home, and it would be easier to pass on hosting. Much easier. But when I remember what it feels like to look around our table at the stories represented, it's always worth the effort. Always.

We think this tradition started in 2007, but we've lost track. A few couples with little ones, whose own families were states and countries away, decided to spend Easter afternoon together. What began one year with the Floods, the Parks, and the Clarks quickly blossomed into what we lovingly refer to as our United Nations Easter. We keep an eye out for anyone who might not have somewhere to go on Easter—or may not even celebrate Easter—but could be interested in being included. On any given Easter, you'll see kurtas, hijabs, spring skirts, and buttoned-down shirts around our table. Palestine, India, Iran, Afghanistan, Indonesia, Mexico, Turkmenistan, Chile, Puerto Rico, Honduras, the Philippines, the United States, and Canada have all been represented over the years.

Easter is our favorite day of the year and central to our faith. What matters the most to us on that day is that we celebrate in grand style, and that we celebrate with who-ever needs a place to belong. We provide the space, but the party comes to life because of those around our table.

I send a text a few days prior. "We can't wait for you to join us on Easter Sunday. Lunch will begin at 1:30 p.m. If you have a favorite cultural dish you'd want to share, feel free to bring it. Or if you're overwhelmed and just want to show up, that's cool, too. We'll have plenty of food. It's gonna be a great day, and we can't wait to celebrate with you!"

People start rolling in after one o'clock in the after-noon, and immediately notice the rises on the stairs that lead up to our 1970s teal front door with its obtuse tri-angle window. After church, Jack takes out the sidewalk chalk and begins adding "welcome" in all the languages represented that particular Easter. On any given year you might see: "*Maligayang Pagdating*," "*Bienvenidos*," "*Ahlan*," "*Selamat Datang*," and "സ്വാഗതം."

Somewhere north of one thirty Jack begins his introduction and we scooch in tight, filling every nook and cranny around the table. People are excited; there are delicious smells—some familiar, some not. There is also a little apprehension as most look around and don't recognize the majority of the people, and no one recognizes everyone. There are multiple faiths represented, with first timers in the crowd, too. Maybe it's their first time at an Easter celebration, or maybe the first time to be in an American home, or maybe, both.

"Welcome! And good news," Jack says. "If you're looking around and see a lot of people you don't know, you're in good company because no one here—not even Alysa and I—know everyone today. So it's perfect—we're all in the same situation."

"We are so excited that you've joined us. Many of you brought yummy food from your homeland that we all get to experience. Wow—what a blessed day! As we like to say around here, a meal shared always tastes better."

"For our family, this day is special for us because we celebrate the death and resurrection of Jesus. For me personally, this frees me from the shame of past mistakes, gives me purpose for how I live today, and hope for my future. Regardless of your faith background, thank you for celebrating with us."

Jack continues, "It is our tradition that we pray and thank God before we eat. Would it be okay if I prayed for lunch?" Jack patiently scans the room before proceeding in prayer, hoping to convey that it truly is okay if someone says they would rather that we not pray.

After prayer, we give quick introductions, ask an ice-breaker question like, "If you could travel anywhere in the world, where would you go?" and then take our plates and head for the smorgasbord we'll remember forever and ever. Amen.

By the time I slide into my chair, the meal is well underway, and every year I take a moment to turn to my left and my right, to see the varied shades, religions, and stories that are wrapped up in striking similarities, too. Aren't we all just people who want to belong to others?

It's a boisterous time—as you might imagine dinner being if you had twenty to thirty siblings. I listen to the layered chitchat as it absorbs the outbursts of laughter and grand storytelling while people settle into conversations with those nearest.

"You're from India? I've never been, but heard it is beautiful. If I ever visit someday, where should I go and what should I do?" *I love that my friends ask thoughtful questions and want to know more.*

"What do you do for a living?" Melissa asks Gabriel.

"When I arrived in Chicago, from Puerto Rico, I needed a job and met a guy who taught me how to work on cars. I've been doing that for about twenty years now," he answers.

They continue talking as I slip a glance in the other direction, only to see our Iranian friend, Tahmina, and our Afghani friend, Fatima, deep in conversation, talking about who knows what. History has separated these countries, but over a meal, they're connecting as new friends. I marvel at the gift of the table, the great equalizer.

For a season, Jack worked at a company where he was one of two white guys, so I laugh as I see Jack's former co-workers tell stories about Jack at the other end of the table, teasing him as he teases them back. At one point, one of them pulls out photos as proof of the time Jack and I entered the "runway contest" at an Indian holiday work party. We came in second. Don't ask.

Across from me and down a few chairs, sits Nour, our dark-haired, olive-skinned Palestinian friend, who had been invited to our table by friends a few years earlier. Occasionally, Easter and Ramadan overlap, and one particular year when they did so, Nour came, brought delicious food to share, and graciously sat visiting with other guests instead of eating. She loved coming to our Easter table and didn't want to miss it, in spite of her own religious holiday that called for fasting until sundown each day during the Ramadan season. To this day, she sends me texts at Christmas, wishing me a Merry Christmas, and regularly sends well wishes on most every other holiday. Nour is extremely thoughtful and kind.

And there, closest to the front windows, Darisa and our neighbor, Mr. John, chat about current global events and that time when John went hunting in Canada. She's a good sport to listen to his tall tales, and I smile at how the world shrinks when we simply extend an invitation.

By this time in the meal, the kids are finished eating and are either outside playing jump rope, hopscotch, or sidewalk chalk art, or have found the game closet in the basement and are playing Uno and Pictionary.

The event lasts most of the day, as people are reluctant to leave. We take a walk around the block to make room for more food, then enjoy desserts from around the world, while tea and coffee keep the conversations rolling.

As the sun starts to disappear, new and old friends help us reassemble our home—happy to contribute as part of the family. When all is said and done, our little family of four ends up lounging on the couch, laughing about moments throughout the day, sharing our favorite snapshots, retelling the tales overheard. Easter evening, I fall into bed absolutely exhausted, with what can only be described as a heart that is filled to overflowing with joy.

The people around our table are among the sweetest gifts I receive every year. If you were to ask about 2020, and the effects the Covid-19 pandemic had on our family, I think we would each say that one of our greatest losses was not hosting Easter that year. The four of us were together, but it just wasn't the same.

We *get* to host a United Nations Easter; it's not a "have to," but a "get to." It is a privilege to carry on this tradition and prepare for others to come in. There is a gift in varied cultures—and religions—eating together around one table. Although our Easter takes extraordinary work, at the end of the day, it's just an ordinary family and eclectic strangers turned friends. We belong to each other through the tradition of an Easter celebration.

Having people over for fancy meals that leave us stressed and anxiety-ridden isn't the type of hospitality I'm generally talking about. But sharing a meal or opening up our homes can be a way we tiptoe into the art of welcome, if we find ourselves curious, wondering where to start.

What if we normalized and prioritized sitting together, and adding more chairs around our tables? It could be as easy as chicken nuggets on paper plates after preschool. Or maybe it is take-out pizza followed by a movie with the new people on the cul-de-sac. Maybe you start a book club and invite a few friends over; you provide the table and they bring the snacks. What if we look for and notice those that might not belong anywhere, and are simply hoping to belong somewhere. Honestly, the invitations to our tables can be some of the most rewarding of all the invitations we'll ever extend.

In Joshua Jipp's book, *Saved by Faith and Hospitality*, he shares something that I come back to over and over again: "…all of us are desperately needy and dependent in every way upon the welcoming and reconciling presence of Jesus."[17] When we see each other as fellow strugglers, all in need of the Welcome Way of Jesus, it flips hospitality on its head. We welcome others because Jesus welcomes us—that's the "why" behind the Imperfect Welcome.

Once the meal is on the table, and I've slipped the napkin onto my lap, my tangible work is done and the ministry of presence takes over. I get to tune in to stories being told. I sometimes interject a funny quip or an added detail to

We welcome others because Jesus welcomes us.

a story, but what I love most is asking questions so that I can hear others share their stories. Whether it is childhood stories or stories of yesterday's work crisis, something sacred happens in the swapping of stories and the passing of green beans.

One day Jesus was asked to narrow down all the commandments—and there are a lot of them—to the most important one. His response? First and foremost, love God with every part of who you are. And a close second? Love your neighbor as you would want to be loved. And if you do these things, you won't be far from the Kingdom of God.[18] Perhaps what I love most about our United Nations Easter tradition is that throughout the day, I feel as if I am very near to the Kingdom of God, where we all long to be. Safe, loved, and known.

10

What Difference Does It Make?

"Don't waste time bothering whether you 'love' your neighbor; act as if you did. As soon as we do this we find one of the great secrets. When you are behaving as if you loved someone, you will presently come to love him."

C.S. Lewis

Eight-year-old Maddie's latest venture was a dog-walking business. It was a win-win. She loved pups and decided she could make a little bit of money by walking them, while also having dog time, which she desperately craved. She created a flyer and off we went, canvassing the neighborhood.

"Mom, can I run a flyer over to that man?"

"Sure. I'll watch from here."

Maddie caught up to the little white dog and his over-sized owner.

"Hi, sir. I started a dog-walking business. Can I walk your dog?" Not giving him a chance to respond, she thrust the paper into his hand, turned, and took off running for home.

"Hey! Little girl, where's your mother?" bellowed the humongous man.

Timidly, Maddie turned and said, while still backing up, "She's just over there, where we live."

"I'll need to talk to her before you can walk my dog because you don't know me. I don't know you, and your mom needs to know who I am."

We met and it was decided. A verbal agreement and a handshake sealed the deal.

"One dollar isn't enough. I'll give you two bucks each time you walk Max because you'll need some hot chocolate money. It's cold outside! And remember to look both ways before you cross the street, especially when you cross the alleys. There are crazy drivers in our neighborhood."

What started out as a question and flyer has become friendship and belonging. He is our Mr. John. Big John. Uncle John.

John is a fun-loving, loud-talking, 6'5" Belgian giant. He happened into our lives because of his little dog, Max, and our little girl, Maddie. Side-by-side, Maddie and Mr. John forged a beautiful friendship through their mutual love of animals, and before long, John sat around our table sharing burgers, potato salad, and stories of life and heartache.

"That girl, she's an angel," he says most every time we're together, and he means it. If you want to know what difference can be made by welcoming someone into your life, look no further than Mr. John.

Born into a strong Catholic family, John's life was characterized by days of mischief, decades of hard-work, and a deep-seeded longing to be loved by his mother. He would share that, of all the difficulties experienced in his sixty-plus years of life, the hardest, bar none, was wondering if his mother Maria loved—or even liked—him. Through countless stories, he reported that Maria was mean-spirited and angry, sending him away from home at any given opportunity. That's not as it should be, and as you might imagine, leaves gaping holes and quiet heartache in the soul of a young boy turned grown man.

> *Sometimes people need a soft spot to land in a lonely, calloused world.*

I'll never forget the first time I heard him step in to correct our child, who was having a meltdown.

"Don't talk to your mother like that. Don't you *ever* disrespect her! You hear me? You have a mom and dad who love you, and you have *no* idea how many people would give *anything* to grow up in your home."

Part challenge, part longing.

Sometimes people need a soft spot to land in a lonely, calloused world.

Over the years, there have been direct confrontations like the one above, yet on more than one occasion, Mr. John would casually and quietly—neither his natural bent—slip in sideways comments like this to our kids. Though decades had passed, he still longed for a mom who loved him.

"I wasn't welcome in my own family, but you welcomed me in," said John.

There's a dance that takes place when you're beginning new friendships. When you let people be who they are, over time and with love and kindness, they become who God means them to be. Our goal shouldn't be to pretty someone up, but rather, to welcome them in.

I look at the gang Jesus chose to be his twelve, go-to guys. Average, every day fellas. I can promise you there were rough edges and yet Jesus said, "Come, follow me."[19] There was no fanfare—he called them as they were.

If Jesus can do that, maybe we can, too?

To John, we were the Cleavers. Something so rare and fantastical—something only fabricated for television. He said, "At first I wondered if you were fake. You actually sit around a table for dinner most nights. Your family just seemed too good to be true. Why would you want to include me?"

John is ... colorful. Larger than life. On plenty more than one occasion we caught ourselves making the cut motion, back-and-forth at our throats, begging him to stop mid-word.

When the visual cue didn't work we would resort to "Mr. John. Little ears."

"So, I took the gun and brought it up to eye-level and…"

"MR. JOHN. LITTLE EARS!"

Whether it is a gruesome hunting story complete with all the gore associated with knife thrusts and bullet wounds, or multiple F-bombs scattered about a colorful retelling of a travel tale, it's part of the package when you welcome people in, right where they are.

Quite frankly, I love it.

He didn't have Sunday School polish. There was no pretense or pretending. As Mr. John says, "You don't have to have your sh*t together to hang with me." John nailed it. None of us is perfect, right? Nor will we ever be.

There is zero "extra" involved in our friendship with Mr. John. He's just one of us. He arrives early for supper, sometimes settling in at our kitchen table while I finish preparing the meal, as we chat about nothing in particular. Other times, Mr. Six-Foot-Five plops down cross-legged on our dirty kitchen floor, hand-feeding green beans to his dog, Max.

"John, I haven't swept in forever. Don't sit there; our floor is filthy."

"Whatever, Alysa. Do I look like I care about dirt? When Max needs to eat, he needs to eat."

And, honestly, John really did not care. At all. He was

feeding his dog with his new family. The setting didn't matter because it was the connection he was after.

Several years running, John, claiming to be "The Great Pumpkin," dressed in a bright orange coat, and joined us as we walked our neighborhood on Halloween. He has been at Jackson's performances, clapping loudest for his solo, wearing his "uncle" badge with pride. He keeps tabs on Maddie's school accomplishments and claims she is the smartest girl he knows. The occasional Friday evening finds him in our basement on family movie nights, laughing together over family favorites like *Cars 2*. We simply told him what many plaques hung over kitchen tables say: "Every family has a story. Welcome to ours."

Invitation. Inclusion. Imperfection.

Connecting is so much more than liking a Facebook post or growing your followers on Instagram. Connection is human. It is face-to-face. And it doesn't take much. Early on in our friendship, especially on days when I didn't particularly feel like having anyone over because I was weary, I remember thinking, *Just show up, Alysa. Show interest. Ask questions. Bring him in.*

Christine Pohl, in her book *Making Room: Recovering Hospitality as a Christian Tradition*, states, "Because eating is something every person must do, meal-time has a profoundly egalitarian dimension. It's the great leveler. Mealtime, when people sit down together, is the clearest time of being with others, rather than doing for others."[20]

John needed somewhere to belong. He didn't *really*

belong to his biological family. Friends had come and gone over the decades. His life was marked by familial hardship which sometimes gave way to poor decisions. Yet there is a kindness in him that runs deep and pops out unexpectedly.

John is tender-hearted underneath that bulky exterior, but those emotions needed to be coaxed out of him. Before kindness could become his new default, he needed a place to belong. He needed the hugs of children and the comfort provided by a table of food and lingering conversation to create a safe space to uncover the deep trauma wound of neglect. Curiosity and attentiveness pushed out the winter detritus, and with the safety of belonging, we were privileged to see new growth emerge.

"Hey John, you should come to church with us."

"Nah! I'm good."

A few weeks later: "John, it's Easter next week. Wanna come to church with us and then over for Easter lunch afterwards?"

"Hmmm. Maybe. I'll think about it."

John declares, "That Alysa! She just wouldn't give up. She kept asking me to come to church every single time I saw her, so finally I just had to say yes to get her off my back. I can't say no to a pretty lady."

Before long, John came to church weekly, sitting in the second row with us, discreetly-not-so-discreetly slipping Jackson candy, riling him up, then chuckling under his breath as Jackson got into trouble. At times we actually separated the two of them (yes, really!). John was soaking it up because he was part of our family.

Our fellow church members and staff started to take a genuine interest in him, too, and what began as Mr. John belonging to us spiraled into Mr. John belonging to others in our church family. He started getting invitations to other tables, and while he never had the mom he longed for, he was starting to have a regular family life. His circle of belonging was enlarging, and it breathed life into his very soul.

> God places the lonely in families.

Psalm 68:6 is worth stating again: "God places the lonely in families, he leads out the prisoners with singing…" Belonging brought the song out of Mr. John's heart that had been buried deep, crusted over with anger and bitterness.

He is a different man today than he was in the early days of our friendship.

The Imperfect Welcome—it works.

His is a tale of underlying sorrow, lost decades of relationship with family members because of deep hurt and an unwillingness to forgive, and yet his slow, steady growth continually unfolds, a transformation worth noting.

"Alysa, I used to be bad. Really mean and angry. But now I've calmed down, and I don't get upset like I used to. I'm willing to talk it out now. Before, my knuckles did the talking for me. Catch my drift?"

John is first to admit that he gave up a lot of rough,

tough, and tumble for Jesus. If we were to view his life as a story, John would say it was a crazy one, one that didn't look like it was headed to a happy ending, and yet he shares now that he is "so grateful that this is the way the ending is turning out."

John landed in jail back in 2007 on a felony charge. Years later, John spotted the man who had ratted him out and landed him in jail those many years prior, walking into an apartment building.

John sat in his car, and waited for the opportune time to exact revenge. At some point hours later, the man walked out of the building with his daughter. In that moment—as the new John, the John who belongs to God—he chose not to retaliate. "The old John would have killed the guy," he said with a somber tone. The new John chose mercy and let the guy live, so that his daughter would not be fatherless.

He chose to let it go.

I asked him what had changed.

"God changed me," he said. "And my little angel, Maddie." God *and* Maddie. "Without the one there *never* would have been the other."

I would argue that the seed of change was planted because one little girl loved his dog and enthusiastically invited Mr. John into her home. Her family showed kindness, and in time, a wider network of new church friends embraced him, which forever changed his life. It's kind of miraculous, really.

Can the Imperfect Welcome be a catalyst for change?

Can old become new? Can an angry heart be softened through the gift of the Imperfect Welcome?

It's possible, friends.

John is a picture of the goodness of God and a pre-arranged divine appointment where strangers met and transformation began. God shows up in the Imperfect Welcome. And while it sometimes feels risky, I have so often been surprised with joy in our ordinary, organic, unlikely friendships. I have been led right to my Heavenly Father because of my friendship with Mr. John.

As much as Mr. John has changed through the gift of the Imperfect Welcome, I've changed, too. My former way of living was subconsciously set against the backdrop of striving for perfection. My focus was on what I could do for God, and how I could do it all. I was exhausted because I was trying to please all the people, busy being who I thought others wanted me to be.

My striving for perfection was, in essence, a longing for deep connection. I wanted to be included, wanted, needed, and ultimately, loved. At some point along the way, I got mixed up, thinking that if I presented myself as having it all together, others would want me. But in reality, perfection does the opposite.

Perfection drives away the connection we're craving because people measure themselves against our *perceived* perfection (remember, we're fooling ourselves if we think we can attain perfection), and they think, "Well, there's no way I'm sharing that struggle with her because she couldn't relate to the hot mess my life is right now." Or, "There's no way I'm inviting her over; she'll die if she sees my small, cluttered home."

For many years I was insecure. Was I enough, just as I was? I wasn't sure, so I strove to do more and be more of who I presumed others wanted me to be. And that's just not an easy—or healthy—way to live.

As it turns out, over time I learned that people want me, not some spruced up version of me. Huh!

What if we traded in the exhaustion (and dare I say loneliness?) that comes from chasing perfection, for the freedom found in being our imperfect selves? And then, what if we welcomed others into our imperfect lives?

Here's what I know. Most people truly do not care what food I serve or how clean my house is, or for that matter, the size of our home. They do not care how well-behaved my children are on any particular day. Most just long for a seat on our sofa. People need to feel that they are welcome, that they belong, and that they are enjoyable to be around. They need someone to open the front door with a smile and a warm greeting, and happily exclaim, "You're here!"

It was probably in the early days of our adventure with Fatima and Abdul, when they would come over every Sunday, for the entire day, that I started to understand this principle. We would cook a meal together and work on her laundry. We would sit and swap stories while the little ones played pretend school, stuffed animals, and launched themselves off the love seat onto the beanbag chair.

Because we spent so much time together, especially that first year, it was impossible to keep up with a perfect home, a perfect meal, and a perfect conversation. It was either: you come over and I just let it go, or, you don't get to come over. And because I longed for her companionship, I slowly started letting things go.

And guess what? I was enough. She didn't care, either. She needed a sister and brother, a niece and nephew.

She needed a family.

And we needed her.

We were two women, born on different continents at about the same time in history. We grew up in wildly different cultures. Hers was a Central Asian experience, and mine was a rural Canadian one. As young girls, joys abounded for both of us; we enjoyed our cultures, our surroundings, and our families. We each reminisce with fondness about picnics, birthday parties, and daily living in the 70s and 80s. In many ways, our similarities outweighed our differences.

Fatima taught me to broaden my perspective and to look for joy in the little things. She taught me to treasure life as it unfolded and to never take it for granted. When I would become impatient because something wasn't going as I had planned, she would put her hand on my forearm and calmly say, "It's okay, Alysa. It's okay." She had a gentle way of redirecting my frustration, reminding me that whatever it was, was not worth getting upset over.

My view of suffering and hardship was challenged. I knew nothing of suffering in comparison to her understanding of hardship, yet she never belittled my mundane mothering woes. She empathized. She understood the weariness that comes from keeping little people fed and clothed. There was room in her story to allow for my hardships, even though, pitted against hers, she could have said, "Oh please. Let me tell you a thing or two of hardship." She was gracious and kind, and she offered a safe environment for me to share my discouragement.

Fatima's arrival to the United States was only a few years after 9/11. Here was a mom with a vastly different story from mine, yet we shared the same hopes, fears, dreams, and concerns. I needed to learn that mothers in Afghanistan desire the same things for their kids as mothers in Chicago.

We have two 1980s brown cloth La-Z-Boy recliners in our basement, and I remember one Sunday afternoon when Fatima and I sat rocking for hours. She shared bits of her hard story, a story of profound loss and exile. After some time, tears streaming, I said, "You're the strongest woman I know."

And she is.

I needed Fatima as much as she needed me. We were just two women longing for connection, in a sometimes dark and lonely world.

11

How Do I Begin?

"The journey of a thousand miles begins with a single step."

Lao Tzu

My garden, if I had one, would be loaded with all the colors of the color wheel, with various textures, shapes, and sizes, mostly wild and free. But the anchor in my garden? Green. Because green in all its shades, offers stability and strength—the very presence of my Heavenly Father.

The bluest of streams would meander through my garden, tumbling over rocks and into the lake just over yonder, alive and refreshing. Jesus, the Living Water, the only One who quenches our thirst, offers himself freely as our living Hope.

The birds would flit about, resting in the strong arms of the maples and the pines, or perhaps on the backs of benches, before darting onto the path to snag worms. They're just there, doing their thing, catching my attention as they fly in and out of focus. They ride the wind, dipping and diving, playful and steady. Similarly, the Holy Spirit carries us toward purpose and fulfillment. Toward each other.

And the flowers. Oh, the flowers. I liken them to you and me, on this journey together. Some are tucked alongside a bench, subtle, steady, and sure. Others stand tall and proud, withstanding the weather, saturated in vibrant violets and pinks. The daffodils spring up out of a cold, dark earth, and faithfully sing their song of newness, while the hardiest of perennials withstand the summer heat. As far as my eyes can see, I spot flower after flower—welcome after welcome—all of us being who we are designed to be.

Somehow, in the belonging to each other—which is the crux of the Imperfect Welcome—growth happens, purpose is found, and love connects what might otherwise stay disconnected.

By its very nature, the Kingdom of God here on Earth is upside-down and counter-intuitive. Somehow, in the belonging to each other—which is the crux of the Imperfect Welcome—growth happens, purpose is found, and love connects what might otherwise stay disconnected. I hope that through the pages of this book you have come to see the value of pursuing a life of welcome, and that you would take your next right step, whatever that might be.

Does the Imperfect Welcome matter?

I know it does.

Isaiah 58:10 says, "…and if you spend yourselves on behalf of the hungry and satisfy the needs of the oppressed, then your light will rise in the darkness, and your night will become like the noonday." Spending ourselves will look different for each of us. For some, it might look like sleepless nights when we're caring for someone else's child. Spending ourselves might also look like volunteering to help a widow at church with lawn care. For others, spending ourselves might be creating a living space above our garage to provide housing for an at-risk teen. Spending ourselves might look like helping the immigrant fill out job applications because job applications are hard enough in one's own language, let alone in a new one. Spending ourselves—**so that God's light rises in the darkness**—shows up in varied ways and usually involves cost, but I wonder if the result outweighs the cost?

So what next?

We move carefully toward others and offer ourselves. Then others move tentatively toward us, offering themselves in return. And in this back-and-forth dance through the garden called belonging, we vulnerably share ourselves in the hopes that we might love one another well.

The people who cross our paths need us. And we need them. When we share who we are—strengths and weaknesses alike—in a way that feels natural and authentic as the person we were created to be, we are living the Welcome Way of Jesus. In the process, hope is produced, joy rises to the surface, and our purpose is enlarged.

When we step into the flow of welcome, change is inevitable. By God's design, we were made to be in community, and joy is available when we enter into relationship with others, especially those deemed different from ourselves. It is in our perceived differences that we are faced with reality; we're really not all that different. People are people the world over, who long for purpose, love, and belonging.

Who captures your heart?

God loves to take our meager offerings—whatever loaves and fish we have—and multiply them beyond our wildest imagination.[21]

You and I were made for this. He calls us to walk toward strangers instead of turning from them. He longs for us to share ourselves, so that in the belonging and connecting, we bring the Kingdom of Heaven down to Earth.

If you were across from me today, I would love to ask you this: if distractions were swept away, if excuses were removed, and if fears weren't ringing loudly in your mind, who captures *your* heart? Who could *you* walk toward? Who needs *you*, just as you are, in all your imperfect ways?

Is it orphans in India or Korea, or is it those struggling with food scarcity in your home town? Is it the man holding the cardboard sign at the intersection, or the refugees who recently arrived in your city? Maybe you work at an elementary school, and you notice the kids sitting alone at lunch and your heart longs to help them belong. Or maybe you were once a single mom and you feel burdened to help other single moms. Do you adore the elderly and want to ensure they aren't forgotten?

Maybe you've walked the cancer road and now have insider knowledge of a world you never wanted, and your knowledge could be a gift to someone with a recent diagnosis. Do you long for kids with special needs to be included in summer parties and baseball leagues? Maybe loneliness and depression have been part of your story and there's a niggling inside of you that wants to turn your pain into a way to help others by heading to graduate school to become a counselor. Perhaps sexual abuse is part of your story and somehow, in some way, you want to fight against the evil of sex trafficking.

Jesus says that when we welcome the stranger, when we care for the needy, and when we offer hope through acts of kindness, it is as if we are doing those very things *to* him and *for* him. I don't understand it, but I know it's true. Somehow, in the reaching across the you're-different-than-me divide, there is a supernatural exchange, and it is as if we are reaching toward the extended hand of Jesus.

I am a better person today for having strangers—who became friends who turned into family—in my life. I can testify that there is an exchange of gifts and a mutual joy wrapped up in the Imperfect Welcome.

I hope you can see it better now.

Acknowledgments

Thank you is a very big deal to me. So much so, that back in 1999, when my husband got down on one knee, and asked, "Will you marry me?" in the excitement of the moment I failed to answer him. Eventually he asked, "So what do you say?" And immediately I said, "THANK YOU!!!!" He replied, "No, to the question, Alysa. Will you marry me?"

As an author (I guess I now get to call myself that!), there is no such thing as writing in a vacuum. This work we do is communal and the stories of my family and friends shaped mine. How can I repay such a gift?

Melissa Parks, we sat across the breakfast table on October 2nd, 2020, me with my list of potential book ideas, and you with your decades of experience, and when we got to *The Imperfect Welcome* idea you said, "That's your book!" You were generous in your help, from that initial brainstorm session to the book we hold in our hands today. You encouraged, you challenged ("Fight for a better way to say this!"), and you believed in me when I didn't think I could do it. I remember thinking, "What do people do if they don't have a bestie in the book-writing business?" I was spoiled on my first writing project because you gave and you gave and you gave. Thank you, dear friend. We did it!

Becky Baudouin, in the middle of the hardest season of my life, God brought us together. I was wounded and not sure I had it in me to start a new friendship or, for that matter, finish a book. Yet, we found ourselves at the lake house for a writing weekend, and I found in you a kindred spirit. God is so good to give us new friends. You have given so much, from reviewing my manuscript (multiple times) to sharing your insights and advice, to being a friend who cares and prays. You were the surprise friend I didn't know I needed. I am so thankful for you.

Dave and Karen Anderson, every bit of this book could be written by you and your family, and Dave, I'm excited that you have a book on hospitality on its way out into the world, too. I'll be the first to buy it! Thank you for modeling what radical hospitality really looks like. You're the real deal.

Joshua Jipp, your endorsement means so much, as someone who has written on the topic of biblical hospitality. While yours is at an academic level and mine is, well, not so much, thank you for cheering me on!

Christina Quist, you've had about as many adventures as I've had, and someday I'd love to hop into your story in South Africa. Thank you for your encouragement, and thanks for such a generous review of my work.

Amy Joob, your endorsement means so much to me, and I'm so grateful for your faithful prayers and encouragement throughout this entire process. What a joy it has been to get to know you this year.

Barb and Paul, Ailie, Jonathan, and Anthony, yours was the family and home I spent the most time in over my three years in Indonesia. You were a safe haven for me and I could have written an entire chapter about our adventures together. You still amaze me.

Nancy and Mel, from the moment you rescued me while I struggled with my first bout of malaria, your small, quiet table reminded me most of my childhood table in Canada. I felt like your daughter, and I needed you. Thank you, sweet friends.

Rosa, Tom, Becca, Kat, and Jonny, you folded me into your loud, crazy family, making heaps of memories together. You'll always be family to me.

Joan, Wally, Jacinda, and Jared, the essence of being a Wiley is to welcome. I smile when I think of each of you. Thank you for scooping me up and inviting me in. You make welcome look easy!

Jakob, Naomi, and Victor, thank you for sharing your parents with me and many others. Gwen and Rog, your door was (and still is) always open. I think I owe you approximately 437 meals. Thank you.

Darissa, you are smart and capable, and I'm so glad our paths crossed those many years ago. We've missed you, but are so delighted to have reconnected in recent days. Thank you for being willing to let me share your story.

My dear Fatima and Abdul: My world became so much brighter the day you arrived. Thank you for being brave and letting me share pieces of your story. I pray that in sharing, many will take steps toward refugees and immigrants. I love you "too" much. And always will.

There are countless people that helped Fatima, and because of her desire for anonymity, I can't list your names, but you know who you are. It took an entire village to welcome her to Chicago. We did it together. You shine so brightly!

Ruth and Ken Haller, and Kristin and Ken Sorensen, the four of you take living out the Christian call to welcome to another level. I've seen it with my own eyes for 20+ years. Thank you for letting me share a sliver of your stories in this book. The ease at which you invite others in, is something to behold!

Tahmina, God was so good to connect us when you arrived in Chicago. After every visit with you I think, "Why don't I see her every single day? She fills my heart with joy!" Continue to be brave and strong. Thank you for letting me share portions of your story in this book. May you continue to sense the nearness of Jesus. I sure do love you and your kids.

Auntie Val, come home for a visit. We miss you so much and love you more. Thank you for letting me stitch together a few threads of your story to encourage others. I am so proud of the woman you have become. Your dependence on God and your love for him is contagious. Stay filled with joy.

Mr. John, I love you like a brother and you will always have a place around our table and in our hearts. I suppose I owe you a lot of potato salad for letting me tell your story. Thank you for saying yes to our Maddie walking your dog.

Catherine and Mark Hankins, please write a book someday because your stories need to be told. I've watched you welcome for years, and you generously, sacrificially, humbly, and faithfully extend invitations to people so that they have a place to belong.

To my faithful cheerleaders: Cleary, Julie, Tina, Tricia, Liz, and too many others to list by name. You texted, you asked how I was, you Marco'd, you took an interest in this project, you jumped for joy when I hit another milestone, and I always knew you were cheering me on. You've each been so kind to me.

Dave Goetz, Melissa Parks, and my writing group (Journey Sixty6): This book would not exist without your encouragement from the very beginning. You believed I could do it, and together, we did! You cheered me on and kept me going! Thank you.

To my early readers: Becky, Dorothy, Cleary, Anna, and Aunt Shirley, you were speedy and you caught mistakes I missed when my eyes were just too close to the project and *The Imperfect Welcome* is better because of you.

To my launch team: I didn't get my act together, so your names aren't printed. I am so sorry about that, but you know who you are. Thanks for being excited with me to launch this book out into the world. Sharing your sphere of influence is helping me to get word out about The Imperfect Welcome. I love each of you and am so grateful for your help.

Becky Skillin, God knew I needed you as my editor and he brought us together in such a beautiful way. In a moment of panic (when I thought I might not get to hire you), I actually cried because I knew that you were the editor for me. I'm so grateful God worked out the timing details so we could crank through these edits this summer. Thank you for pushing hard to make this dream happen. We did it. Whew!

David Edelstein, you came highly recommended as a book designer, and now I know why. Thank you for working to meet my ridiculous deadline. You are efficient and talented, and I'm so grateful for your expertise. I think the book looks great!

Ron, Cindy, Nicole, and René (Brideau), I understand welcome at the soul level because of the four of you. Thank you for making us part of your family. I have no words and I love you so much.

And on behalf of the 140+ foster children who have been welcomed into your home, thank you for your decades of service.

> It has been a long time since I've lived in Canada, but northern Ontario is filled with families who invited us in. Uncle Dean and Aunt Dolly, I spent almost as many hours at your home as I did my own. I'm sorry about all the times I spilled milk all over your table. And to the Tullochs, Scotts, and Smiths, your extended families helped me feel like I had grandparents, aunts, uncles, and cousins. And to every other family that welcomed us in—I am so grateful for your generosity. You are family.

Alice, your family took me in when I was an international college student, unable to go home for holidays. My love of all things Chicago and Chicagoland started with you. The Art Institute, The Chicago Symphony Orchestra, Ravinia, and on and on I could go. Your family gave me a place to belong, and for that I am forever grateful.

> Denise and Michelle, as I reflect back over my life, our memories over the decades are among my favorites. You are the sisters I never had and you have welcomed me into your hearts my whole adult life. I will forever thank Jesus that he gave us to each other.

Papa, you welcomed me into the Clark family as if I was your very own. I'm sitting here looking out at the lake—your favorite place—as I type these words. How fitting. I'll miss you until heaven, when we see each other again.

Becky Jo, you gave me the use of your beautiful "tree-house" back in April 2022, which enabled me to write for a month—what a gift! And, you're on your own journey of welcoming immigrants to the United States. You are a fierce and faithful advocate for so many. I love you!

Aunt Shirley, I marvel at your natural ability to invite others in and make them feel at home. You are filled with grace and kindness and so many have been the recipients of your welcome, including me and my family. I love you so much!

Lenny and Sarah, you live a life of welcome and my heart bursts with sisterly pride over how you consistently open the door to your home, fridge, pantry, and lives. You are selfless and faithful. Thank you for living a life of welcome. Many in your neighborhood, church, and sphere of influence, belong to you. You inspire me more than you know. I love you!

Dad, tag you're it—now it's time to finish your book! I'm cheering you on because the world needs your words on the Psalms. I love you so much and pray for many more years of memories together.

Mom, your example of what it means to love Jesus has encouraged me my entire life. Thank you for praying me through this project, and thank you for believing I could do it. Thanks, too, for sharing your seamstress skills, making countless bookmarks and bags for my book launch. You love me so well and you're the best mama a girl could ask for. I love you!

Maddie and Jackson, my hope and prayer would be that both of you would always have room around your tables to share a meal with others, especially those that land on the fringes of society. I long for you to continue to have eyes to see those that need an invitation and continue to be intentional in your welcome.

Maddie, my heart explodes with delight over the young woman you have become. Your curiosity got us into a lot of these stories, so for that, I am forever indebted. From the time you were little you have noticed those who need a friend and I pray that continues your whole life. Keep growing in your love for Jesus. Sweet sweets, I love you with every part of my heart.

Jackson, my heart explodes with joy over the young man you are becoming. You have a way of making others feel welcome wherever you go. You are loyal and kind, just exactly what the world needs. Keep chasing Jesus, Buddy. I love you with every part of my heart.

Jack, you are adventurous and funny, and there is nobody I would rather do life with than you. You have never met a stranger and that is one of the things I love most about you. I love my book cover that you designed and it is all that I hoped it would be. Your edits helped shape this book into what we hold in our hands today. It is exactly what it needed to be and wouldn't have been so without your input. This is our book, our heart, and together, we're always better. I wonder who we'll meet next? I love you and I like you!

Heavenly Father, I've said from the beginning that this is "our book." You carried me through the process. "You are my God, and I will give you thanks; you are my God, and I will exalt you. Give thanks to the LORD, for he is good; his love endures forever." (Psalm 118:28-29)

One Last Thing

This book isn't about the Clark family
and their adventures.

This book is about how one yes, and then another,
and then another, transformed us and
those around us while we saw Jesus provide
abundantly despite our limitations.

And if we can do it—
one ordinary family in Chicago—
then you can, too.

Please realize that any good
you see on these pages is Jesus.

Notes

1. Safe Families for Children: https://safe-families.org/

2. Rift Valley Academy: https://rva.org/

3. Hillcrest School: https://hismk.org/

4. World Relief Chicagoland: https://chicagoland.worldrelief.org/about-us/

5. Luke 10:25-37

6. While people have their preferences, Lou Malnatti's is most definitely the best deep-dish pizza in Chicago: https://www.loumalnatis.com/

7. Mark 12:28-34: Author's paraphrase

8. Matthew 25:35

9. 2 Corinthians 9:7

10. Romans 12:13

11. Breakthrough: https://breakthrough.org/

12. Mothers of Preschoolers (MOPS): https://www.mops.org/

13. Isaiah 40:11

14. Third-culture kid: https://www.merriam-webster.com/words-at-play/third-culture-kid

15. Jeremy Courtney, Justice Conference, June 14, 2017, Willow Creek, South Barrington, Illinois.

16. Matthew 25:40

17. Jipp, Joshua W. *Saved by faith and hospitality*. Chicago: Wm. B. Eerdmans Publishing Co., 2017. (page 36)

18. Mark 12:28-34: Author's paraphrase

19. Matthew 4:19

20. Pohl, Christine D. *Making room: Recovering hospitality as a Christian tradition*. Grand Rapids, MI: W.B. Eerdmans, 1999. (page 74)

21. John 6:1-14

Appendix A:
From Mother Teresa

I never look at the masses as my responsibility. I look only at the individual. I can love only one person at a time. I can feed only one person at a time. Just one, one, one. You get closer to Christ by coming closer to each other. As Jesus said, "Whatever you do to the least of my brethren, you do it to me." So you begin...I begin. I picked up one person... The whole work is only a drop in the ocean. But if we don't put the drop in, the ocean would be one drop less. Same thing for you. Same thing in your family. Same thing in the church where you go. Just begin...one, one, one! At the end of our lives, we will not be judged by how many diplomas we received, how much money we have made or how many great things we have done. We will be judged by "I was hungry and you gave me to eat. I was naked and you clothed me. I was homeless and you took me in.

Taken from the book "Michel Collopy, Works of Love Are Works of Peace; Mother Teresa of Calcutta and the Missionaries of Charity" (San Francisco: Ignatius, 1996). 35

Appendix B:
What Kids are Saying

I asked several kids (most of whom are now adults), whose parents faithfully live a life of hospitality, to send in a few sentences about the impact it had on them to live in a home that regularly welcomed others in. Here's what they had to say:

Ailie (41): "My parents have always welcomed people into our home, whether it was for a meal, a holiday, or for months at a time. Our lives are richer because of the relationships that were cultivated through sharing a meal, talking, playing games, creating memories, and laughing. Witnessing my parents' generous hospitality has made it a natural thing for me to want to welcome people into our home."

Ezra (10): "We have a lot of people come to our house so I learn to get along with lots of different kinds of people, and get practice playing with lots of different ages of kids."

Jacinda (43): "My parents (who were missionaries on a remote island in Indonesia), had an open-door policy which brought people from all walks of life to our dinner table. I always helped cook and set the table—pulling together the best of what we had: sometimes a simple casserole, sometimes a catch-of-the-day from a recent beach excursion, and always some sort of dessert that my mom whipped up. But the food was never the focus. Etched in my memory is the feeling of anticipation and connection that came at dinner time. We prayed together and then the most fascinating discussions would ensue. We heard stories of what brought National Geographic travelers to search for hidden caves deep in the mountain jungles, we grieved with local friends whose family members suffered from malaria and TB, we heard colleagues talk of how God was at work in the midst of serious challenges. We all—no matter our age—entered into the discussions. I learned to listen, to empathize, and to laugh with others. I saw how God was at work, whether or not we had the same faith background as those who ate with us. I saw generosity, kindness, goodness, and joy. I learned cross-cultural communication and I practiced sharing resources and stewarding time, especially when a stranded traveler or troubled teenager stayed for months at a time. I saw love in action as my parents beautifully modeled hospitality."

Katie (33): "Growing up, my parents invited people into our home often—sometimes for a few hours for a meal, sometimes it was weekly dinners, Bible studies, or an invitation to stay the night on their way to the airport, stay the week if it was needed, or even stay six months if necessary.

As a young child I remember feeling loved by many people who came into our home, sometimes feeling frustration for the "boring" meetings that were being held in the living room, and feeling joy as we shared moments with strangers who became friends. I believe my parents were not only giving to others when they opened up their home, but they were opening up doors of love to us, their children. We were loved by these strangers, cared for, played with, and taught. We have so many "aunties" and "uncles" all over the world who still love us. Now, as an adult, I see how intentional you have to be to host, to be hospitable, and to share your home with others. It is not always an easy task, but it is rewarding and beautiful."

Raychel (32): "Having an open home taught me to be less self-focused. Learning to share, scoot over, and listen to other people's stories taught me to look beyond myself and my personal issues, and to realize that everyone is going through something. It also taught me that everyone needs a home, even the strongest people need a place to relax and let their hair down."

Zeph (13): "It's not always easy to have lots of people in our house and it can be awkward at first, but it gives me a chance to practice manners and I learn how to build relationships."

About the Author

Alysa Clark is a story-driven author and speaker. After graduating with a master's degree in teaching, Alysa taught in Indonesia for a season—an adventure of a lifetime. Currently, she lives in Chicago with her husband, Jack, and their two children, Madison and Jackson. They enjoy exploring national parks, traveling abroad, and stumbling into cross-cultural experiences.

A Blessing

"The LORD bless you and keep you;
the LORD make his face shine on you
and be gracious to you;
the LORD turn his face toward you
and give you peace."

Numbers 6:24-26

Made in the USA
Monee, IL
22 August 2023